This book is dedicated to everyone on *Main Streets* all around the world – including the

- ❖ *Billions living in poverty around the globe*
- ❖ *Almost 100 MILLION unemployed Americans*
- ❖ *Underemployed*
- ❖ *Homeless*
- ❖ *Retired*
- ❖ *Veterans*
- ❖ *Military personnel*
- ❖ *Teachers*
- ❖ *Homemakers*
- ❖ *Students*
- ❖ *...*
- ❖ *and to anyone who wishes to generate some extra income!!*

< i >

Other books by Iris Marie Mack, Phd, EMBA

Energy Trading and Risk Management: A Practical Approach to Hedging, Trading and Portfolio Diversification (Wiley Finance) 1st Edition

Mama says, "Money Doesn't Grow on Trees!" (World of Dr. Mackamatix Mathematics Edutainment Book)

< ii >

CONTENTS

< iii >

Chapter 2

Chapter 3

Chapter 4

< vi >

PREFACE

I learned a lot while researching and writing this book – too many items to list here. However, one of the most amazing things I learned was from talking to students in several *Masters of Finance* (MFIN) programs at a few major universities. They told me that their professors hardly – if ever – mentioned the role the Federal Reserve (the U.S. Central bank) plays in our monetary system. At first, I thought these students were pulling my leg. So, I asked one of them to make an appointment with one of her finance professors and explicitly ask this professor about the Federal Reserve. The student said her meeting resulted in ZERO information from this finance professor about the U.S. Central bank – just a few minutes of mumbo jumbo and then *let me get back to you* (which never happened by the way).

Keep in mind that many of these MFIN students end up working in financial institutions on Wall Street or in other financial centers around the globe. Now you have to stop and ask yourself the following question:

> *If Masters level students studying Finance at major American universities are not taught about the role the Federal Reserve plays in our monetary system, what hope is there for the average person on Main Street to be able to wrap their brains around this mysterious entity and understand how it affects their lives in so many ways?*

This amazing revelation about finance education in the U.S. immediately brought to mind the following quote from a speech by our late President John Fitzgerald Kennedy (Kennedy, 1961).

> *"The very word 'secrecy' is repugnant in a free and open society; and we are as a people inherently and historically opposed to secret societies, to secret oaths and to secret proceedings."*

< vi >

You're probably wondering – who cares! What does the Federal Reserve have to do with this book? I know, right. You came here to learn how to make money; get your bailouts; learn how to do this so-called *bulletproof trade* we mention in our sub-title. So, no need to worry, we will get to all of this. Please bear with us. There are a few important matters we need to discuss – such as the Federal Reserve – to help you understand how to get paid with a bulletproof trade.

0.1 LIGHT BULB GOES OFF: BULLETPROOF TRADING STRATEGY

Over the past few years, I've taught courses on energy trading and risk management – on a university level, for executive courses on Wall Street, in Europe, and Asia. Whenever I lectured and conducted trading labs on the bulletproof trading strategy discussed and illustrated in this book, I noticed a transformation in many of my students. It's like a light bulb turning on in their heads. They seem to sit up, take notice and lean in to soak up what I am trying to impart. It is simply fascinating to look out into the trading lab and/or lecture halls to observe this.

Eventually, I got the idea to start talking about this bulletproof trading strategy with relatives, friends, colleagues, and even some strangers – to get their reaction. Surprisingly, theirs was almost the same reaction as many of my students. Some even got angry and would ask, *"Why the heck hasn't my broker told me about this?"*.

Several people have gone so far as to ask, and some even demand, that I tutor them on this trading strategy. A few asked if I would take a bit of money from their portfolios and do some trades on their behalf in my personal portfolio. A couple of them even started to read my recently published energy trading book (Mack, 2014) to try to learn more about this trading strategy. However, to their chagrin, this book was a bit too technical for several of them. So, this is why I decided to write this how-to book about this bulletproof trading strategy for the laypersons – based on some of the more technical concepts presented in my energy trading book.

< vii >

My co-authors and I have lots of experience with this bulletproof trading strategy – academically, professionally, and in our own personal portfolios. In addition, we had a chance to battle test this bulletproof trading strategy during the recent Brexit-related market volatility (Wheeler, 2016). So, for us, this bulletproof trading strategy is not just academic. It is the real deal because it helped us make money and protected us from downside risk after the markets dropped shortly after the UK decided to exit the European Union. By the time you finish reading this book, you should be able to use this bulletproof trading strategy to get some Main Street bailouts from Wall Street too!

0.2 OVERVIEW OF THE BOOK

Some of the key features of this book are the numerous examples, case studies, trading screen shots, and illustrations of a bulletproof trading strategy that will help you get paid – immediately!

The structure of the chapters in this book is as follows:

Chapter 1: Introduction – Financial crisis of 2007-2009, Bank Bailouts, Federal Reserve, "Rent" Stocks, Covered Call Options, Unemployment "Math," TradeStation, Covered Call Checklist, www.MainStBailout.com

Chapter 2: Bank Bailouts from Main Street and the Federal Reserve - U.S. Department of Treasury, Troubled Asset Relief Program (TARP), Federal Reserve, Federal Reserve Bailouts to Domestic and Foreign Banks

Chapter 3: Main Street's Bailout - Derivatives, The Derivatives Pyramid, Bailouts, Bail-ins

Chapter 4: Stock Options - Options Contract, Call Options, Put Options, Options Trading Strategies, TradeStation Options Symbols, Buy Call Option Strategy, Sell Call Option Strategy

< viii >

< ix >

ACKNOWLEDGMENTS

I would like to acknowledge the help of all the people and organizations involved in this book project.

- ❖ **Co-Authors** – Some of my former students and/or teaching assistants in my Energy Trading classes at the Tulane Freeman School of Business: Jiacheng Fu (Aaron), Xiaogang Han (Miami), Xuyan Shi (Sarah) and Jingyuan Xue (Wilson)
- ❖ **Professional Editor** – Wayne H. Purdin
- ❖ **Graphics Artist** – Mohammad Asif of *JaZaa Financial Advisory*
- ❖ **Book Cover Illustrator** – Jose Julian Ramirez Rivas
- ❖ **Professional Indexer** – Jessica McCurdy Crooks of *Next Index Services, LLC.*
- ❖ **TradeStation Securities, Inc.** – Educational Director Jesus Nava allowed us to use trading accounts and market data to develop case studies and examples for our book.
- ❖ **Book Reviewers** – Gustavo Ayala; Pye Ian, MBA; Alexei Kazakov, PhD; Michael C. Thomsett, PhD; David Trevino, MBA; Cheng Wang, MBA

Without the hard work, patience, support, and dedication of these individuals and organizations, this book project would not have become a reality.

< x >

ABOUT THE AUTHOR

Iris Marie Mack, PhD, EMBA, earned a doctorate in Applied Mathematics from Harvard University. She was also awarded a Sloan Fellowship Executive MBA from the London Business School. Dr. Mack worked at various energy and financial institutions, acted as a faculty member at MIT, and worked at NASA and AT&T Bell Labs – where she obtained a patent for research on optical fibers.

Dr. Mack currently lectures on Energy Trading and Risk Management for the Fitch Learning *Certificate in Quantitative Finance* Program on Wall Street and at Tulane University. Because of Dr. Mack's extensive knowledge of the derivatives, energy trading and investment banking world, she has been invited to write opinion columns for the UK edition of the *International Business Times*.

Dr. Mack has also been named one of *Glamour Magazine*'s Top 10 Working Women, and she is no novice writer. This publishing will be her third financially-focused and published book – including her energy trading book published with Wiley Finance and a financial literacy book for teens and adults. With this breadth of experience and sheer intellectual prowess, Dr. Mack is more than able to help readers reach the financial stability they deserve (Mack, 2004; Mack, 2011; Mack, 2014)

In addition, Dr. Mack founded *The Global Energy Post and MathQED* - a homework help site for K-12 and college students. Previously known as Phat Math, this service has even been named one of the *Top 50 Social Sites for Educators and Academics, 25 Savvy Social Media Sites for Grad Students and 25 Useful Networking Sites for Grad Students.* Such accolades illustrate Dr. Mack's ability to clearly inform the masses. (Learn-O-Rama, 2016; OnlineMastersDegree, 2011; PhDProgramsOnline, 2011)

< xi >

ABOUT THE CO-AUTHORS

Co-Author	Bio
Jiacheng Fu (Aaron)	**Jiacheng Fu** earned a Master in Finance in 2015 and Master of Management in Energy in 2016 – both at Tulane University. During his studies, he worked as a teaching assistant for Dr. Iris Mack's *Energy Fundamental and Trading* class. Currently Mr. Fu is running *Lize Big-Data Asset Management* company. This is an Asset Management and IT service company for the Finance and Energy industries. His firm focuses on trading strategy design. Mr. Fu co-authored Chapter 4.
Xiaogang Han (Miami)	**Xiaogang Han** earned a Master of Finance at Tulane University. After graduation, he chose to work in China. Now he serves Shanghai Huatong Silver Exchange. He is in charge of trading, risk management, derivatives design and settlement for the exchange. He has passed CFA Level 1 and FRM Part 1 and is preparing for the next level. Mr. Han co-authored Chapters 5 and 6.
Xuyan Shi (Sarah)	**Xuyan Shi** earned a Master of Finance at Tulane University in 2016. During her studies, she worked as a teaching assistant for Dr. Iris Mack's *Energy Fundamental and Trading* class. After graduation, Ms. Shi interned at ClipperData LLC as an Energy Data Analyst in New York City. There, she was in charge of analyzing North American energy companies' financial and production data. Ms. Shi co-authored Chapter 2.
Jingyuan Xue (Wilson)	**Jingyuan Xue** earned a Master of Management in Energy at Tulane University in 2015. After earning his degree, he chose to return to China to work at China Huaneng Group - the largest power group in the world. Currently Mr. Xue focuses on Chinese and global carbon trading markets and renewable energy project investments. Mr. Xue co-authored Chapter 7.

< xii >

REFERENCES

President John Fitzgerald Kennedy, *John F. Kennedy Speeches*, http://www.jfklibrary.org/Research/Research-Aids/JFK-Speeches/American-Newspaper-Publishers-Association_19610427.aspx, 1961.

Learn-O-Rama, *Top 50 Social Sites for Educators and Academics*, http://www.dualmasters.org/top-50-social-sites-for-educators-and-academics.html, 2016.

Mack, Iris Marie, *Mama says, "Money Doesn't Grow on Trees!"* Xlibris, https://www.amazon.com/Mama-says-%20Money-Doesnt-%20Trees-%20ebook/dp/B00DH9NY5E?ie=UTF8&keywords=iris%20mack&qid=1464219653&ref_=sr_1_4&sr%20=8-4, 2004.

Mack, Iris Marie, *Mama says, "Money Doesn't Grow on Trees!"* Createspace, https://www.amazon.com/Mama-says-%20Money-Doesnt-%20Trees/dp/1456502905/ref=sr_1_5?ie=UTF8&qid=1464219653&sr=8-5&keywords=iris+mack, 2011.

Mack, Iris Marie, *Energy Trading and Risk Management: A Practical Approach to Hedging, Trading and Portfolio Diversification*, Wiley Finance, Singapore, https://www.amazon.com/Energy-Trading-Risk-Management-Diversification/dp/1118339339/ref=sr_1_1?s=books&ie=UTF8&qid=1473991942&sr=1-1&keywords=iris+marie+mack, 2014.

OnlineMastersDegree, *25 Savvy Social Media Sites for Grad Students*, http://onlinemastersdegree.org/25-savvy-social-media-sites-for-grad-students/, 2011.

PhDProgramsOnline, *25 Useful Networking Sites for Grad Students*, http://www.phdprogramsonline.org/25-useful-networking-sites-for-grad-students.html, 2011.

Wheeler, Brian and Alex Hunt, "Brexit: All You Need to Know About the UK Leaving the EU," *BBC*, http://www.bbc.com/news/uk-politics-32810887, 2016.

< xiii >

CHAPTER 1

INTRODUCTION

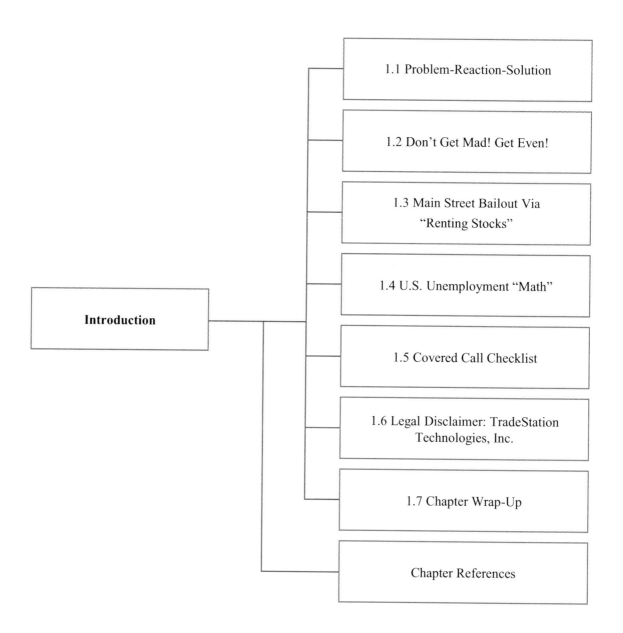

Introduction

- 1.1 Problem-Reaction-Solution
- 1.2 Don't Get Mad! Get Even!
- 1.3 Main Street Bailout Via "Renting Stocks"
- 1.4 U.S. Unemployment "Math"
- 1.5 Covered Call Checklist
- 1.6 Legal Disclaimer: TradeStation Technologies, Inc.
- 1.7 Chapter Wrap-Up
- Chapter References

< 1 >

CHAPTER 1

INTRODUCTION

1.1 PROBLEM-REACTION-SOLUTION

To set the framework for our book, we will borrow from what is known as the *Hegelian Dialectic*. This is a methodology created by Georg Wilhelm Friedrich Hegel, a 19th-century German philosopher. The Hegelian Dialectic is commonly expressed in its simplest form as "Problem-Reaction-Solution" (Parrish, 2014). More explicitly, an *"agent of change"* employs the Hegelian Dialectic:

1. Creates a ***problem*** or crisis
2. Foments the ***reaction***
3. Attempts to control the outcome by providing   the ***solution***

As has been documented in numerous books, academic papers, news articles, movies, etc., the financial crisis of 2007-2009 led to very large bailouts for banks and some insurers. We summarize this financial crisis and subsequent bailouts using the Hegelian Dialectic framework in Figure 1.1 (Elliott, 2011; Huddleston, 2015).

Figure 1.1: **Financial Crisis of 2007-2009 and Bank Bailouts**

PROBLEM	REACTION	SOLUTION
The financial crisis of 2007-09 was considered to have been the worst financial crisis since the Great Depression of the 1930's.	Treasury Secretary Hank Paulson, Fed Chairman Ben Bernanke, etc. said this financial crisis threatened the collapse of "Too Big to Fail" Banks and other financial institutions.	Bailouts for domestic banks, international banks and other financial institutions (courtesy of U.S. taxpayers): 1.Billions of dollars in bailouts from the U.S. Treasury Department 2.Trillions of dollars in bailouts from the Federal Reserve

< 2 >

While many people may be aware of the billions of dollars in bank bailouts from the U.S. Treasury Department, they are perhaps unaware of the trillions of dollars in bank bailouts from the Federal Reserve. In Chapter 2, we will discuss these bank bailouts in great detail in layperson's terms.

1.2 DON'T GET MAD! GET EVEN!

I think most people will agree that the bank bailouts did very little to help the *99%* of people on Main Street. Even though I may find myself getting irritated from time to time about the poor and middle class bailing out the rich bankers, I decided to be proactive instead and help Main Street try to get some bailouts too.

When people ask me to briefly describe the bulletproof trading strategy discussed in this book, I usually jokingly tell them two words – *Highway Robbery!* In addition, what I am about to teach can be summarized in the following three steps:

1. What I am about to teach you in this book is indeed *legal*! Why? Because Wall Street pays its bankers, lobbyists, and lawyers to go to Capitol Hill to make the laws to ensure that what bankers do is indeed legal (Dayen, 2015).

2. The trading strategy I am about to teach you in this book is also very good. I mean, after all, Wall Street traders at Goldman Sachs utilize this trading strategy and their CEO LLoyd Blankfein says they're just *doing God's work!* (Phillips, 2009).

3. What I am about to teach you is how to trade a certain type of financial contract and to *make money ASAP.*

But before I do all of this, I need to define and illustrate a few financial markets and trading concepts in subsequent chapters. Look, the average folks on *Main Street may as well help themselves to a piece of the Wall Street pie* now, so they won't be so mad about more bank bailouts (and/or bail-ins) when the music stops, the party is over, and the markets collapse again (Berger, 2016).

Don't get mad! Get even! Stop wasting precious time getting mad at Wall Street bankers, and just get even. Learn some of their "legal" conservative trading strategies and play on their turf. Once you do, you will have more power and more money to improve your and your family's economic situations. Why should Main Street let the Wall Street bankers have all the fun and roll in the dough! Come on; get in on the action too!

1.3 MAIN STREET BAILOUT VIA "RENTING STOCKS"

Many stock investors buy stocks with the hope they will increase in value – not to just languish idly in their portfolios. However, not all stock investments generate profits as quickly as we would like them to. But no need to worry. The stock investor may utilize shares that are experiencing slow or stalled growth to generate additional returns by "renting" these idle shares of stocks. These stock rentals help to provide liquidity to the stock market – ensuring that there are enough sellers and buyers.

Simple Analogy: Savvy real estate investors would never leave their vacant real estate properties idle. They would do everything possible to lease or rent these properties to generate revenues. In a similar manner, stock investors can also "rent" stocks in their portfolios – by utilizing the bulletproof trading strategy we discuss in this book.

In Figure 1.2, you'll find a schematic diagram of what we plan to discuss and illustrate in the subsequent chapters: *rent your stocks by trading covered call options*. These type of options allow an investor to generate extra cash flow in his/her portfolio. The strategy is so safe, in fact, that it is suitable for most retirement accounts. By the time you finish reading this book, you will agree that the covered call options strategy is indeed bulletproof!

< 4 >

Figure 1.2: Main Street Bailout Via "Renting Stocks"

PROBLEM	REACTION	SOLUTION
• Trillions in bailouts for domestic banks, international banks and other financial institutions (courtesy of U.S. taxpayers) • Unemployment • Bankruptcies • Homelessness, Depression, Suicide…	• Read this book • Study, practice, and apply what you learn	Main Street Bailout = Rent your stocks by trading "covered call options"

1.4 U.S. UNEMPLOYMENT "MATH"

A few years ago, I wrote a short article about some of the creative analytical methodologies employed by economists and statisticians at the *Bureau of Labor Statistics* (BLS) to calculate the official U.S. unemployment rate. (Mack, 2011) Essentially, each month the U.S. government reports some very interesting unemployment "math" – as illustrated in this example.

Example: On October 7, 2016, the BLS reported its monthly unemployment data – summarized in Table 1.1.

Table 1.1: *U.S. Unemployment 'Math' (October 7, 2016)*

Americans "Participating" in Labor Force	Americans NOT "Participating" in Labor Force	"Official" Unemployment Rate
159,907,000 (out of 254,091,000 Americans 16 or older)	94,184,000 (out of 254,091,000 Americans 16 or older)	
62.9%	37.1%	5.0%

< 5 >

On one hand, the BLS announced with great fanfare that the "official" unemployment rate was 5.0%. However, on the other hand, it reported that 37.1% of Americans 16 or older were not "participating" in the labor force.
Note: The BLS determines a person to be "participating" in the labor force if he/she is either holding a job or actively seeking one. (Jones, 2016)

You're probably wondering why do I bring up this BLS data? Well, it's safe to say that many people on Main Street could use a bailout - especially the 37.1% of Americans who were NOT "participating" in the labor force in October 2016. So, if these 94,184,000 Americans have access to a computer and the internet, then many of them can learn how to use the trading strategy discussed in this book to acquire new skills and perhaps make some money as well.

1.5 COVERED CALL CHECKLIST

By the time you finish this book, you will have a blueprint for how to rent your stocks to an exchange and to collect some bailouts on a regular basis. If you are new to the financial markets, we recommend you study this book one chapter at a time. In addition, you may wish to work with a partner or in some type of investment or book club.

To facilitate your learning process, from time to time, we will provide various resources and financial literacy information from our website www.MainStBailout.com. In particular, one of the tools we provide from www.MainStBailout.com is a *Covered Call Checklist*. This checklist will be a great tool for investment clubs, book clubs, individual investors, traders, teachers, students, workshop facilitators, homemakers, senior citizens, single parents, veterans... basically anyone or any group that is serious about learning how to get some Main Street bailouts from Wall Street.

< 6 >

1.6 LEGAL DISCLAIMER: TRADESTATION TECHNOLOGIES, INC.

TradeStation has granted us legal permission to use screen shots, data, and trading case studies in this book. The techniques and methods described in these screen shots and case studies illustrate best practices. However, no investment or trading advice, recommendation, or opinions are being given or intended. All rights reserved.

1.7 CHAPTER WRAP-UP

In this chapter, we gave readers some motivation for the bulletproof trading strategy to be discussed and illustrated in this book. To accomplish this task, we discussed:

- ❖ The Hegelian Dialectic: Problem-Reaction- Solution
- ❖ The financial crisis of 2007-2009
- ❖ Bailouts for Wall Street and Main Street
- ❖ Bulletproof trading strategy: "renting stocks"
- ❖ Covered call options strategy
- ❖ Unemployment "math"
- ❖ TradeStation legal disclaimer
- ❖ Covered call checklist
- ❖ www.MainStBailout.com

< 7 >

REFERENCES

Berger, Rob, "How to Prepare for the Coming Stock Market Crash," *Forbes Magazine*, http://www.forbes.com/sites/robertberger/2016/07/29/how-to-prepare-for-the-coming-stock-market-crash/#693f0c21327a, 2016.

Dayen, David, "Wall Street Pays Bankers to Work in Government and It Doesn't Want Anyone to Know," *New Republic*, https://newrepublic.com/article/120967/wall-street-pays-bankers-work-government-and-wants-it-secret, 2015.

Elliott, Larry, "Global Financial Crisis: Five Key Stages 2007-2011", *The Guardian*, https://www.theguardian.com/business/2011/aug/07/global-financial-crisis-key-stages, 2011.

Huddleston, Tom, Jr., "These 7 Movies Tell the Real Story Behind the Financial Crisis," *Fortune Magazine*, http://fortune.com/2015/12/27/big-short-wall-street-movies/, 2015.

Jones, Susan, "94,184,000 Not In Labor Force; Labor Force Participation Rises; Unemployment Rate Ticks up to 5.0," *CNS News*, http://cnsnews.com/news/article/susan-jones/94184000-not-labor-force-labor-force-participation-rises, 2016.

Mack, Iris, "Unemployment 'Math': Statistical Lies," *Huffington Post*, http://www.huffingtonpost.com/iris-mack/unemployment-math-statist_b_819783.html, 2011.

Parrish, Brent, "Hegelian Dialectics for Dummies," *The Right Planet*, http://www.therightplanet.com/2014/01/hegelian-dialectics-for-dummies/, 2014.

Phillips, Matt, "Goldman Sachs' Blankfein on Banking: 'Doing God's Work,'" *The Wall Street Journal*, http://blogs.wsj.com/marketbeat/2009/11/09/goldman-sachs-blankfein-on-banking-doing-gods-work/, 2009.

< 8 >

CHAPTER 2

BANK BAILOUTS FROM MAIN STREET AND THE FEDERAL RESERVE

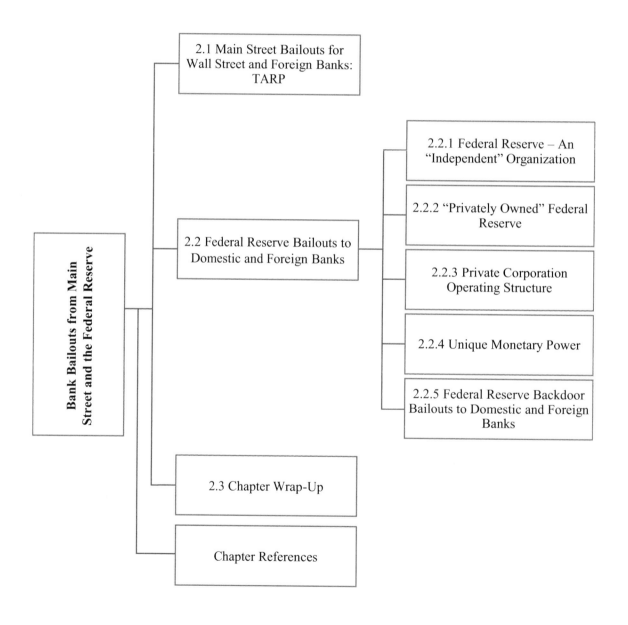

Bank Bailouts from Main Street and the Federal Reserve

2.1 Main Street Bailouts for Wall Street and Foreign Banks: TARP

2.2 Federal Reserve Bailouts to Domestic and Foreign Banks

2.2.1 Federal Reserve – An "Independent" Organization

2.2.2 "Privately Owned" Federal Reserve

2.2.3 Private Corporation Operating Structure

2.2.4 Unique Monetary Power

2.2.5 Federal Reserve Backdoor Bailouts to Domestic and Foreign Banks

2.3 Chapter Wrap-Up

Chapter References

< 9 >

CHAPTER 2

BANK BAILOUTS FROM MAIN STREET AND THE FEDERAL RESERVE

2.1: MAIN STREET BAILOUTS FOR WALL STREET AND FOREIGN BANKS: TARP

Since the subprime mortgage crisis in 2008, the U.S. government has provided money to hundreds of banks, a few insurers, and automakers as part of the $700 billion Troubled Asset Relief Program (TARP).

Since the subprime mortgage crisis in 2008, the U.S. government has provided money to hundreds of banks, a few insurers, and automakers as part of the $700 billion **Troubled Asset Relief Program** (TARP). Some firms have repaid the government, and many have announced they intend to return the money (Ericson, 2009).

In Figure 2.1, we present a summary of the TARP bailout recipients.

Figure 2.1: **TARP Bailout Breakdown (Ericson, 2009)**

COMMITTED $549.4 Billion										UNCOMMITTED $150.6
Financial firms,not returned $79.3	Citigroup $50	Bank of America $45	A.I.G $69.8	Automakers,GMAC $85.3	Homeowners $50	Small business $15	Public-Private $100	TALF $55	Unused $80.5	Returned $70.1

< 10 >

TARP bailout program is officially called the Emergency Economic Stabilization Act of 2008.

This TARP bailout program is officially called the *Emergency Economic Stabilization Act of 2008*. (Emergency Economic Stabilization Act, 2015) Consultations among Treasury Secretary Henry Paulson, Chairman of the Federal Reserve Ben Bernanke, U.S. Securities and Exchange Commission Chairman Christopher Cox, Congressional leaders, and President Bush, moved forward efforts to draft a proposal for a comprehensive solution to the problems created by illiquid assets. News of the coming plan resulted in some stock, bond, and currency markets stability on September 19, 2008 (Emergency Economic Stabilization Act, 2008).

Until 2011, 43 cents of every dollar spent by U.S. government was borrowed, four times the rate in 1980.

A lot of people thought the money for the TARP bailout came from the U.S. taxpayers and the government's borrowing. Until 2011, $0.43 of every dollar spent by U.S. government was borrowed, four times the rate in 1980. Between 2007 and 2011 alone, the rate had increased to $0.38 per dollar. In other words, the U.S. government borrowed more and more to bailout those big banks but made nothing better for the average person (de Rugy, 2011). With the huge cost, what the government hoped to get from the bailout was, basically, aid to the big banks that held the mortgage lenders' debt. Then this was supposed to help circulate cash in the economy and help investors regain confidence in the banking system.

Derivatives

Table 2.1 shows the assets and total exposure to *derivatives* liabilities of five major banks in the U.S. It's clear these "Too Big To Fail" banks have at least 30 times more derivatives exposure on their financial statements than assets (Snyder, 2015). Is another crisis on its way?

Table 2.1: *Assets and Derivatives Liabilities of Some "Too Big to Fail" Banks*

	Total Assets	Total Exposure to Derivatives
JP Morgan Chase	$2.6 Trillion	$63 Trillion
Citibank	$1.8 Trillion	$59 Trillion
Goldman Sachs	Less Than $1 Trillion	$57 Trillion
Bank of America	$ 2.1 Trillion	$54 Trillion
Morgan Stanley	Less Than $1 Trillion	$38 Trillion

< 11 >

The most recent estimate of the U.S. national debt is $19 trillion dollars (U.S. National Debt Clock, 2016).

One glaringly obvious question is this: does the U.S government have the resources to continue to bail out troubled corporations, banks, and insurance companies? Many investors, taxpayers, and economists don't think so. Since 2008, the U.S. has become overextended, with trillions of dollars in debt. Hence, it no longer has the resources to fund such huge bailouts in the future (Davis, 2008). The most recent estimate of the U. S. national debt is $19 trillion dollars (U.S. National Debt Clock, 2016).

Moreover, the huge cost of these bailouts didn't offer that much benefit for the economy, investors, and definitely not for U.S. taxpayers (Boyd, 2012). Unfortunately, the "Too Big To Fail" banks are getting bigger and bigger since the government bailouts in 2008. As a result of these bailouts and the ongoing seemingly endless recession, many banks lost the public trust (Newman, 2011). In addition, since the economy has never been properly repaired after the previous economic collapse, many experts think that we're due for an even bigger economic collapse in the future. So, what will the government do next time around? How will the banks be bailed out? Also, who will bail the rest of us out? Investors? Small businesses? The average taxpayers on *Main Street*?

The most recent bank asset concentration statistics are shown in Figure 2.2. Clearly, we see continuously high concentration levels, and it seems the trend will not end any time in the near future (FRED, 2015).

Figure 2.2: **Five Bank Asset Concentration for U.S.**

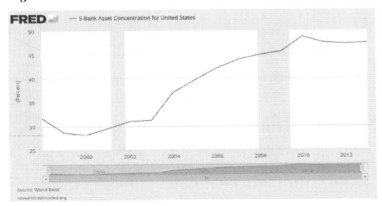

< 12 >

The bailouts in 2008 have also been politically unpopular, with many critics insisting that governments should not intercede in the dynamics of a free market. In addition, many believe that the role of governments is to take care of the investors' and bank customers' interests (Nielsen, 2008).

In May 2010, in an attempt to subdue the burgeoning fiscal crisis in Greece, the EU and IMF extended a 110 billion Euros ($120 billion dollars) bailout package.

Bailouts didn't only take place in the United States. There were also bank bailouts in the Euro Zone (Katz, 2010). In May 2010, in an attempt to subdue the burgeoning fiscal crisis in Greece, the EU and IMF extended a €110 billion Euros ($120 billion dollars) bailout package in exchange for the Greek government to agree to implement austerity packages equal to 14 percent of Greece's GDP. In August 2015, Euro-area finance ministers signed off on a bailout program for Greece for as much as €86 billion Euros ($95 billion dollars), paving the way for the nation to attempt to pay its bills and begin rebuilding its economy (Christie, 2015). The *sovereign debt* crisis kept the Euro Zone away from a sustainability union for future stable growth (European Sovereign Debt Crisis, 2009). The repayment of billions in bailouts is beyond expectation. Without any positive progress resulting from the bailouts, the Greek economy will continue to collapse and investors will suffer again and again.

Sovereign Debt

Sovereign debt refers to bonds issued by a national government in a foreign currency, in order to finance the issuing country's growth. (Sovereign debt definition, Investopedia)

Can individual investors and/or average people on Main Street benefit from these Wall Street bailouts? Unfortunately, it seems that for many, the answer is NO. Since 2008, millions of people have lost their jobs, homes, pension plans, savings, and any hope for a brighter future for younger generations. Billions of people and investors are angry and feel a sense of hopelessness. Such emotions are understandable for a while, but perhaps counterproductive in the long run. You don't need to get mad. Get even! You can learn a few tricks of the trade to make some of that Wall Street money for yourself! That's right. In subsequent chapters we will discuss how to make the Wall Street bailouts benefit those on Main Street!

< 13 >

2.2: FEDERAL RESERVE BAILOUTS TO DOMESTIC AND FOREIGN BANKS

In the remainder of this chapter, we will discuss the secret backdoor bailouts that domestic and foreign banks received from the Federal Reserve. However, before we can do that, we need to spend a bit of time discussing what exactly the Federal Reserve does and how it is structured.

2.2.1: FEDERAL RESERVE -- AN "INDEPENDENT" ORGANIZATION

You may have been surprised when you read the title of this section. You may have thought: *Shouldn't the Federal Reserve be a government department?* I bet most people hold the same thought as you do. Unfortunately, the answer to this question is ------ **NO!** **Here are several samples of how some experts view the Federal Reserve**:

For over a century, the Federal Reserve has operated in secrecy, to the benefit of the elites and the detriment of the people. (Paul, 2015)

The Federal Reserve System is not Federal; it has no reserves; and it is not a system, but rather, a criminal syndicate. It is entirely private-owned, although it seeks to give the appearance of a governmental institution. (Mullins, 1983)

The Federal Reserve is a key component of the American Transfer State. Under the guise of "macroeconomic management," it redistributes vast amounts of wealth on an ongoing basis through inflation. The victims of these transfers are ordinary Americans. The beneficiaries are the government and its elite cronies. (Sanchez, 2016)

> *For over a century, the Federal Reserve has operated in secrecy, to the benefit of the elites and the detriment of the people. (Paul, 2015)*

< 14 >

The Federal Reserve makes it very clear on its official website that it works as an **independent** entity, not controlled by either executive or legislative branches of the U.S. government. It also specifically states on its website that: "It [Federal Reserve] is **NOT 'owned'** by anyone and is **NOT a private, profit-making** institution. " ("Who owns the Federal Reserve?" *Board of Governors of the Federal Reserve System*, 2013).

In the remainder of this chapter, we will peel off the Fed's guise step by step. Let's analyse the underlying structure of the Federal Reserve in different aspects.

2.2.2: "PRIVATELY OWNED" FEDERAL RESERVE

One of the most important things that muddy the discussion of the "ownership" of the Federal Reserve is that the regional Federal Reserve banks issue stocks to its "member banks."

Regional Federal Reserve Banks

Definition of ***Regional Federal Reserve*** **banks:** A substantial piece of the Federal Reserve System consists of the 12 regional Federal Reserve Banks located around the country: including Atlanta, Boston, Chicago, Cleveland, Dallas, Kansas City, Minneapolis, New York, Philadelphia, Richmond, San Francisco and St. Louis. (Figure 2.3) These 12 regional Federal Reserve Banks were established by Congress to operate as the arms of the nation's central bank. (Federal Reserve Act, 1913)

Figure 2.3: **Twelve Regional Federal Reserve Banks (Federal Reserve Bank, 2016)**

< 15 >

Member Banks

Definition of ***Member Banks***: The Federal Reserve Act requires all nationally chartered banks to join the Federal Reserve system by purchasing the capital stocks of the Federal Reserve Bank for that district. But for the state chartered banks, the Federal Reserve gives them the option to join the system, which means all the state chartered banks can decide whether or not to become one of the "member banks" themselves. The amount of stocks that a member bank is required to purchase is proportional to the size of the bank. (Federal Reserve Act, 1913)

In other words, the way to join the Federal System and become a member bank is to be a shareholder or an owner of the regional Federal Reserve Bank. The bigger the commercial bank is, the larger the number of shares it owns!

Example of a *Member Bank*: Suppose a new national bank opens in New Orleans, Louisiana. For the sake of this example, we call it *BankNOLA*. The Federal Reserve Bank of Atlanta's New Orleans branch office is located at 525 St. Charles Avenue in New Orleans. It's one of the five branch offices of the Federal Reserve Bank of Atlanta. So, in order to do business as a commercial bank in New Orleans, *BankNOLA* has to join the Atlanta Federal Reserve Bank System by purchasing a certain amount of stocks of the Atlanta Fed, being one of the "owners." Moreover, shares required to purchase depend on the size of *BankNOLA*. Hence, *BankNOLA* will become one of the shareholders of the Atlanta Federal Reserve Bank.

< 16 >

Clearly, Eustace Mullins saw through the *smoke and mirrors* of the Feds and, as discussed in his book *The Secrets of the Federal Reserve*, Mullins states that the Federal Reserve is entirely privately-owned under its guise of a governmental institution. (Mullins, 1983) In addition, he reported who the top eight stockholders of the New York Fed were at that time:

1. Citibank
2. Chase Manhattan Bank
3. Morgan Guaranty Trust
4. Chemical Bank
5. Manufacturers Hanover Trust
6. Bankers Trust Company
7. National Bank of North America
8. Bank of New York

According to Mullins, these American institutions in 1983 owned a combined 63% of the New York Fed's stock. However, most of those American banks listed above, in fact, are owned by about a dozen European banking organizations, mostly British, and the most prominent one among them is the Rothschild banking dynasty. Since the member banks of the New York Fed elect their board of directors, The London Connection, a European banking club, is able to pick the Fed's directors through the American banks they own and, ultimately, control the entire Federal Reserve System. (Mullins, 1983)

If you have doubts about Mullins's theory, let's look at what the Fed itself says. The New York Fed reports that its eight largest member banks, that is, its biggest stockholders, on June 30, 1997 were:

1. Chase Manhattan Bank
2. Citibank
3. Morgan Guaranty Trust Company
4. Fleet Bank
5. Bankers Trust
6. The Bank of New York
7. Marine Midland Bank
8. Summit Bank

< 17 >

After about 14 years, these two lists are not exactly the same. However, five of the eight banks from the 1983 list were on the 1997 list, proving the validity of Mullins' argument in his book.

In conclusion, the regional Federal Reserve bank is privately owned by its member banks and indirectly controlled by various European financial institutions through ownership of the member banks.

2.2.3: PRIVATE CORPORATION OPERATING STRUCTURE

The Fed is considered an independent central bank because its decisions do not require any approval from the President of the United States nor from anyone else in the executive or legislative branches of the U.S. government.

The Fed is considered an independent central bank because its decisions do not require any approval from the President of the United States nor from anyone else in the executive or legislative branches of the U.S. government. The Fed was created to be autonomous and isolated from day-to-day political pressures. For example, members of the Board of Governors are appointed to serve a 14-year term, outlasting many presidential and congressional terms. (Board of Governors of the Federal Reserve System, 2015)

In addition, according to the *Federal Reserve Act* Section 7, the capital stock of the Federal Reserve bank pays a fixed 6% dividend and gives the shareholders a claim on the Fed's annual profits. (Federal Reserve Act, 1913) A mere 6% a year may not be considered a large profit in the Wall Street world. However, most businesses that manage to cover all their expenses and give their shareholders a guaranteed 6% return are considered "for-profit" corporations. It seems like the Federal Reserve's "not-for-profit" slogan is not valid.

Short Case Study: In 2014, the Federal Reserve's total distribution of net income was $99.6 billion, $1.7 billion of which was paid out for dividends on capital stocks and $96.9 billion of which was remitted back to the U.S. Treasury. (The Federal Reserve Annual Report of 2014) Compared to $99.6 billion, $1.7 billion doesn't seem like a very big number. But think about it! $1,700,000,000 is the dividend that this "corporation" paid out! Yes, and the Federal Reserve claims to be a "non-profit organization."

< 18 >

Another thing that makes the Federal Reserve Banks' "ownership" status confusing is its operating structure. The 12 regional Federal Reserve Banks operate more like private corporations with each having its own nine-member board of directors. (Figure 2.4) Six of these directors are elected by the member banks of the respective Federal Reserve District and the other three directors are appointed by the Board of Governors. Most Federal Reserve Banks have at least one branch, and each branch has its own board of directors. Most of the directors on a branch board are appointed by the Federal Reserve Bank, and the remaining Branch directors are appointed by the Board of Governors. This System structure is exactly the same as a private corporation. (Board of Governors of the Federal Reserve System, 2013)

Figure 2.4: **Federal Reserve Board of Director and Corporate Structure**

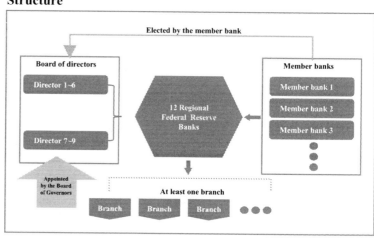

2.2.4: UNIQUE MONETARY POWER

< 19 >

It [Federal Reserve] has the right to print and issue money, the traditional prerogative of monarchs. It is set up to provide financing for wars. It functions as a money monopoly having total power over all the money and credit of the people. (Mullins, 1983)

It [Federal Reserve] has the right to print and issue money, the traditional prerogative of monarchs. It is set up to provide financing for wars. It functions as a money monopoly having total power over all the money and credit of the people. (Mullins, 1983)

The *Bureau of Engraving and Printing* (BEP), a division of the U.S. Treasury is responsible for printing the U.S. currency and delivering the money to the Fed. Each year, the BEP prints billions of Federal Reserve Notes for delivery to the Fed. Then the Fed has to decide how much money to circulate into the economy ultimately—no approval required from the President of the United States or the Congress needed. (Hamrick, 2013) Moreover, the Federal Reserve has become much more technologically creative in modern society. The money no longer has to be physically presented in daily transactions now. Most businesses and consumers rely on checks, debit and credit cards, and balance transfers for transactions. Therefore, money creation doesn't have to be physical either. In other words, the Fed can simply create new money by typing numbers into certain accounts on a computer. (Money Creation, 2016)

The most frequent monetary policy tools the Fed utilizes are *Open Market Operations.*

Open Market Operations

Definition of *Open Market Operations* (OMO): The OMO refers to the central bank buying and selling financial assets such as treasury bills, government bonds, or foreign currencies from private parties, like commercial banks. Purchasing these assets results in currency entering market circulation, while selling these assets removes circulating currency. Usually, open market operations are used to target a specific short-term interest rate. (Money Creation, 2016)

The timing and the quantity of Treasury bonds the Fed purchases or sells totally depend on the Fed itself. No other department, institution, or individual can control this process.

< 20 >

Let's take a look at a case study of how the Federal Reserve circulates money into the U.S. economy.

> ***The Government's Shell Game*** (Figure 2.5): Suppose the U.S. government needs a certain amount of money, let's say $200 million, to cover its current expenditures (bureaucrat salaries, military weapons purchases, welfare payments, etc.). Since the public has a limited tolerance for taxation, the U.S. Government, who we'll refer to as Uncle Sam in this case study, has to call upon the Federal Reserve to use its money-printing powers.

> First, Uncle Sam asks the Treasury to issue bonds to investment banks, like Goldman Sachs, to raise the money he needs. Issuing bonds is essentially equivalent to writing on a piece of paper: "IOU $200 million." Then, Goldman lends the government money by purchasing bonds. Goldman transfers $200 million to Uncle Sam's ledger and, in return, Uncle Sam gives Goldman a piece of paper as $200 million Treasury bonds, which represents that the Treasury owes Goldman $200 million plus interest. When Uncle Sam gets this $200 million, he will use it to pay the bills by writing checks or transferring money to other accounts. The money goes from Goldman to Uncle Sam, then to the public to whom Uncle Sam owes money. This is essentially how the money is circulating in the economy.

> At this point the Federal Reserve enters the shell game. Now the Fed finds out that Goldman Sachs is selling $200 million Treasury bonds and intends to purchase the bonds. So the Fed pays $205 million to Goldman for the bonds plus a little bit of profit. But the Fed uses its own way of paying, which is by simply writing "Debit $205 million cash" directly on Goldman's ledger. Goldman now has $205 million deposit into its account at the Federal Reserve, $200 million principal and $5 million profit. At this point, $205 million enters the market because Goldman will use the money in its normal business, like loaning it to clients.

< 21 >

Afterwards, every time that Goldman withdraws money from its account at the Federal Reserve, the Fed delivers newly printed money to Goldman. In this way, the new money printed by BEP finds its way to circulate in the economy. For the present, Goldman is done with this game, but Treasury ends up owing the Fed money, the principals of the bond and interests. (Sanchez, 2016)

But the tricky thing is, remember that the Fed contributes all of its profits to Treasury at the year-end. In other words, interests and principals the Treasury pays back to the Fed will be handed back to the Treasury as the Fed's profits. It's just like moving your money from the left pocket to the right pocket, and then moving it back!

Now, let's sort out this Shell Game in Table 2.2 and Figure 2.5:

Table 2.2: *The Government's Shell Game*

Shell Game Participant	Before	After
U.S. government	Needs $200M to cover expenses	Receives $200M to cover expenses
Treasury	Issues $200M bonds (Prints out paper)	Owes $200M to the Fed (Fed gives its profits back to Treasury.)
Goldman Sachs	Lends $200M	Receives $205M
Federal Reserve		Buys bond from Goldman Sachs. (Types $205M on Goldman's ledger) Treasury owes the Fed $200M and the interest.
Market		$205M new money enters U.S. economy

< 22 >

In conclusion, the government doesn't pay anything. The Treasury doesn't pay anything, and the Fed doesn't pay anything! But $205 million has been circulating in the markets and Goldman gets $5 million as profits. This is how **inflation** is created! The amount of goods in the market is the same, but the amount of money in circulation used to buy the goods has increased. Therefore, more money will be needed to buy the same goods than before. However, in the short term, the workers' salaries won't necessarily be increased accordingly. This is how our money is devalued, while Uncle Sam and Goldman both come out richer! The U.S. taxpayers are the **victims** of this Shell Game!

Figure 2.5: **The Government's Shell Game**

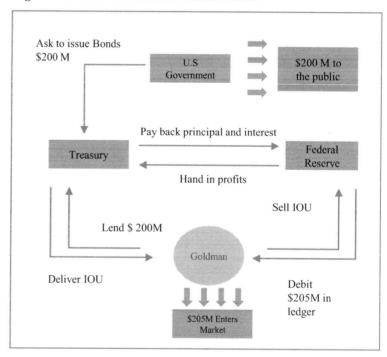

After all the things we have discussed thus far, do you still think the idea of the Federal Reserve being an independent organization is too far-fetched?

< 23 >

2.2.5: FEDERAL RESERVE BACKDOOR BAILOUTS TO DOMESTIC AND FOREIGN BANKS

Now that we have spent a bit of time discussing what the Federal Reserve does and how it is structured, we will now take a look at its secret backdoor bailouts to domestic and foreign banks.

What we present in this next couple of paragraphs and table may absolutely astound many of our readers. After the subprime mortgage crisis in 2008, the Federal Reserve secretly conducted the biggest bank bailout in the history of the world. To make matters worse, the Fed fought in court for several years to keep these bailouts a secret from the U.S. taxpayers. Many taxpayers remember the multibillion dollars TARP bailout, discussed in the beginning of this chapter. Folks on Main Street are still very angry that the U.S. government spent hundreds of billions of dollars bailing out "Too Big To Fail" Wall Street banks. Well, the TARP bailout was a fraction of the "bailouts" the Federal Reserve gave to domestic and foreign banks.

As detailed in Table 2.3, the Federal Reserve gave more than $16 trillion dollars in nearly interest-free money to many "Too Big To Fail" domestic and foreign banks between 2007 and 2010. This multi-trillion bailout was revealed during a limited GAO audit of the Federal Reserve, mandated by the Dodd-Frank Wall Street Reform and Consumer Protection Act. (Greenstein, 2011) Just to put this number in some perspective, keep in mind that the GDP of the U.S. for the entire year of 2010 was only $14.58 trillion dollars. In addition, the total U.S. national debt is currently over $19 trillion dollar and still counting. (Snyder, 2011; Snyder, 2016; Webster, 2011)

< 24 >

Table 2.3: *Bailouts from the Federal Reserve to Domestic and Foreign Banks (Webster, 2011)*

Dollar in billions

Borrowing Parent Company	TAF	PDCF	TSLF	CPFF	Subtotal	AMLF	TALF	Total loans
Citigroup Inc.	$110	$2,020	$348	$33	$2,511	$1	-	$ 2,513
Morgan Stanley	-	1,913	115	4	2,032	-	9	2,941
Merrill Lynch & Co.	0	1,775	166	8	1,949	-	-	1,949
Bank of America Corporation	280	947	101	15	1,342	2	-	1,344
Barclays PLC (United Kingdom)	232	410	187	39	868	-	-	868
Bear Stearns Companies, Inc.	-	851	2	-	853	-	-	853
Goldman Sachs Group Inc.	-	589	225	0	814	-	-	814
Royal Bank of Scotland Group PLC (United Kingdom)	212	-	291	39	541	-	-	541
Deutsche Bank AG (Germany)	77	1	277	-	354	-	-	354
UBS AG (Switzerland)	56	35	122	75	287	-	-	287
JP Morgan Chase & Co.	99	112	68	-	279	111	-	391
Credit Suisse Group AG (Switzerland)	0	2	261	-	262	0	-	262
Lehman Brothers Holdings Inc.	-	83	99	-	183	-	-	183
Bank of Scotland PLC (United Kingdom)	181	-	-	-	181	-	-	181
BNP Paribas SA (France)	64	66	41	3	175	-	-	175
Wells Fargo & Co.	159	-	-	-	159	-	-	159
Dexia SA (Belgium)	105	-	-	53	159	-	-	159
Wachovia Corporation	142	-	-	-	142	-	-	142
Dresdner Bank AG (Germany)	123	0	1	10	135	-	-	135
Societe Generale SA (France)	124	-	-	-	124	-	-	124
All other borrowers	1,854	146	14	460	2,475	103	62	2,639
Total	**$3,818**	**$8,951**	**$2,319**	**$738**	**$15,826**	**$217**	**$71**	**$16,115**

2.3: CHAPTER WRAP-UP

In this chapter, we discussed some of the recent bailouts to banks made at the U.S. taxpayers' expense:

❖ The billions of dollars in bailouts to domestic banks made via the TARP program were discussed in section one of this chapter.
❖ The trillions of dollars in secret backdoor bailouts to domestic and foreign banks from the Federal Reserve were discussed in section two of this chapter.

To accomplish this task, we illustrated how the Federal Reserve is a "privately owned" bank. Unfortunately, the ultimate victims of these bailouts is **"US"**, the average taxpayers. So, please continue reading the remainder of this book to learn how to use the bulletproof "Covered Call Options" trading strategy to help protect yourselves from the U.S. government's and Federal Reserve's reckless spending! We teach you, step by step, how to make the most profits with the least risk so that you folks on Main Street can get a bailout from Wall Street.

< 25 >

REFERENCES

Board of Governors of the Federal Reserve System, "Membership of the Board of Governors of the Federal Reserve System, 1914-Present," http://www.federalreserve.gov/aboutthefed/bios/board/boardmembership.htm, 2014.

Board of Governors of the Federal Reserve System, "What does it mean that the Federal Reserve is "independent within the government"?," http://www.federalreserve.gov/faqs/about_12799.htm, 2015.

Board of Governors of the Federal Reserve System, "Who owns the Federal Reserve?," http://www.federalreserve.gov/faqs/about_14986.htm, 2013.

Boyd, J. H., & Heitz, A., "The social costs and benefits of too-big-to-fail banks: A "Bounding" Exercise," http://casee.asu.edu/upload/TBTF_AER_Final_New_Title.pdf, 2012.

Christie, R., "Euro area agrees on 86 billion-euro bailout deal for Greece," *Bloomberg,* http://www.bloomberg.com/news/articles/2015-08-19/euro-area-agrees-on-bailout-deal-for-greece-eu-commission-says, 2012.

Davis, M., "Top 6 U.S. government financial bailouts," http://www.investopedia.com/articles/economics/08/government-financial-bailout.asp, 2008.

de Rugy, V., "How much of federal spending is borrowed for every dollar?," http://mercatus.org/publication/how-much-federal-spending-borrowed-every-dollar, 2011.

Emergency Economic Stabilization Act of 2008, https://en.wikipedia.org/wiki/Emergency_Economic_Stabilization_Act_of_2008, 2015.

Emergency Economic Stabilization Act of 2008, Pub. L. No. 110–343 § 122 STAT. 3765, https://www.gpo.gov/fdsys/pkg/PLAW-110publ343/pdf/PLAW-110publ343.pdf, 2008.

Ericson, M., He, E., & Schoenfeld, A., "Tracking the $700 billion bailout," *The New York Times,* http://www.nytimes.com/packages/html/national/200904_CREDITCRISIS/recipients.html, 2009.

"European Sovereign Debt Crisis," *Investopedia,* http://www.investopedia.com/terms/e/european-sovereign-debt-crisis.asp, n.d.

Federal Reserve Act, 1913, "Federal Reserve Bank," *Wikipedia,* https://en.wikipedia.org/wiki/Federal_Reserve_Bank, 2016.

< 26 >

Flaherty, Edward, "Who owns and controls the Federal Reserve," http://www.usagold.com/federalreserve.html, 2001.

FRED, "5-bank asset concentration for United States," https://research.stlouisfed.org/fred2/series/DDOI06USA156NWDB, 2015.

Greenstein, Tracey, "The Fed's $16 Trillion Bailouts Under-Reported," *Forbes,* http://www.forbes.com/sites/traceygreenstein/2011/09/20/the-feds-16-trillion-bailouts-under-reported/#1241bd4e6877, 2011.

Hamrick, Mark, "5 myths debunked about the Federal Reserve," http://www.bankrate.com/finance/federal-reserve/myths-federal-reserve-1.aspx, 2013.

Katz, A., & Martinuzzi, E., "Greek deals hidden from EU probed as bonds show doubt," *Bloomberg,* http://www.bloomberg.com/news/2010-09-07/greek-debt-deals-hidden-from-eu-probed-as-400-yield-gap-shows-bond-doubts.html, 2010.

Lebor, A., "The Eurozone's death by a thousand bailouts," *Newsweek* http://www.newsweek.com/2015/08/14/death-thousand-bailouts-359147.html, 2015.

"Money creation," *Wikipedia,* https://en.wikipedia.org/wiki/Money_creation, 2016.

Mullins, Eustace, *The Secrets of the Federal Reserve*, 1983.

Newman, R., "Why you should worry about a "TARP Moment." http://www.usnews.com/news/blogs/rick-newman/2011/07/12/why-you-should-worry-about-a-tarp-moment, 2011.

Nielsen, B., "Economic meltdowns: Let them burn or stamp them out?," *Economic Meltdowns: Let Them Burn or Stamp Them Out?*, 2008.

Paul, Ron, *Don't be Fooled by the Federal Reserve's Anti-Audit Propaganda,* http://www.ronpaulinstitute.org/archives/featured-articles/2015/march/08/don-t-be-fooled-by-the-federal-reserve-s-anti-audit-propaganda/, 2015.

Political Research Associates, "Myth #5. The Federal Reserve is owned and controlled by foreigners," http://www.publiceye.org/conspire/flaherty/flaherty5.html, n.d.

Quintieri, David, *The Money GPS: Guiding You Through An Uncertain Economy*, 2012.

Roche, Cullen, "Here's Who Actually Owns The Federal Reserve," http://www.businessinsider.com/who-actually-owns-the-federal-reserve-2013-10, 2013.

< 27 >

Sanchez, Dan, "Understanding the Federal Reserve's Shell Game," https://mises.org/library/understanding-federal-reserve%E2%80%99s-shell-game, 2016.

Snyder, M., "Have You Heard About The 16 Trillion Dollar Bailout The Federal Reserve Handed To The Too Big To Fail Banks?," http://theeconomiccollapseblog.com/archives/have-you-heard-about-the-16-trillion-dollar-bailout-the-federal-reserve-handed-to-the-too-big-to-fail-banks, 2011.

Snyder, M., "The six too big to fail banks in the U.S. have 278 trillion dollars of exposure to derivatives," http://theeconomiccollapseblog.com/archives/the-six-too-big-to-fail-banks-in-the-u-s-have-278-trillion-dollars-of-exposure-to-derivatives, 2015.

Snyder, M., "Trump is Right – Here Are 100 Reasons Why We Need To Audit The Fed," http://www.thetradingreport.com/2016/02/24/trump-is-right-here-are-100-reasons-we-need-to-audit-the-fed/, 2016.

"Sovereign Debt," *Investopedia*, http://www.investopedia.com/terms/s/sovereign-debt.asp, n.d.

The Federal Reserve Annual Report of 2014, 2014.

U.S. National Debt Clock: Real Time., http://www.usdebtclock.org, 2016.

Webster, S.C., "GAO Fed Investigation," http://www.scribd.com/doc/60553686/GAO-Fed-Investigation#outer_page_144, 2011.

< 28 >

CHAPTER 3

MAIN STREET'S BAILOUT

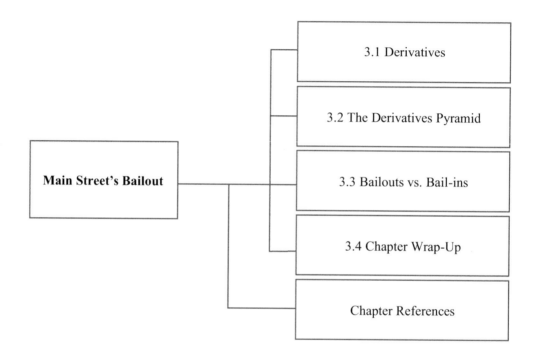

< 29 >

CHAPTER 3

MAIN STREET'S BAILOUT

One of the favorite topics in my energy trading classes is the **Covered Call Options** strategy. Well, maybe it's just one of my favorites, and my poor students have no say in the matter. They have to like it if they want to pass my class. Just kidding! Anyway, I asked my very sharp students to explain the risks and benefits of a covered call option strategy to a teenager. They came up with so many clever and humorous ways to do this. For example, here's how my MBA student Arjun Sreekumar breaks it down:

> **Arjun**: Hey kid. A covered call options strategy is a great way to make money. Basically, this strategy involves
>
> ❖ Buying shares of a stock – also known as *going long* these shares of stock.
>
> ❖ Simultaneously writing a call option – also known as selling a call option, or *shorting* a call option.
>
> Just keep in mind that a call option gives you the right but not the obligation to buy a stock in the future for a certain "exercise" price.
>
> **Teenager:** What are the benefits and risks of a covered call option strategy?
>
> **Arjun**: The main benefit of writing a covered call option is that it is an income-generating strategy. Think of it like this: an exchange is paying you money to hold onto a stock that you already own. A covered call strategy will work well if the price of the stock rises slightly or stays the same. While you can have heavy losses from writing covered calls if the price of the stock falls significantly, the maximum gain can also be very high. The maximum gain will basically be the premium collected from writing a call option plus the difference between the "exercise" price and the stock price at expiration.

< 30 >

Teenager: Can I write covered calls in my Roth IRA retirement account?

Arjun: Yes, you can. And the huge advantage of writing covered calls in a retirement account as opposed to a traditional brokerage account is that when you reach retirement age, you can withdraw the profits made from covered call writing tax free. That means Uncle Sam won't touch a penny!

Teenager: Gee thanks, Arjun! I'm going to go watch MTV and sit in my room and complain about life now.

Arjun: Stay in school, kid!

This dialogue between Arjun and the teenager sums up what we plan to discuss from here on out in this book—the income-generating covered call options strategy. You can think of this strategy as a way to generate Wall Street bailouts for Main Street. However, before we can formally define and illustrate Main Street's bailouts, we need to set the foundation by presenting a few definitions and discussing a bit of technical jargon about the options market.

3.1 DERIVATIVES

Stocks are fairly well known to most people. They constitute fairly straightforward investments. However, an option is a different animal. It is a class of financial derivatives, based on (or derived from) another underlying financial asset. As (Mack, 2014) explains, the term *derivatives* has been tossed around quite a bit over the past few years (p. 34). So what are derivatives?

Derivatives

Definition: A ***derivative*** is a type of financial security whose price is dependent upon or derived from the value or return of one or more assets. The assets that provide the pricing base for a derivative are defined as the *underlying assets* of the derivative.

< 31 >

Laypersons' translation: Derivatives are financial bets made on assets that investors may not necessarily own, but allow them to earn income off these assets.

In Chapters 3 and 4 of (Mack, 2014), one can find definitions, illustrations, and discussions of various types of derivatives. Then, in subsequent chapters, one finds applications of these derivatives to hedge (manage) price risk and to speculate or gamble. For more on the theory of derivatives, see (Mack, 2014) and (Wilmott, 1998).

3.2 THE DERIVATIVES PYRAMID

Please recall that in Chapter 2, we discussed the trillions of dollars in bank bailouts from the U.S. Treasury and the Federal Reserve. As large as these bailouts seem, they pale in comparison to the value of outstanding derivatives contracts. Well-known blogger, Michael Snyder asks: *When is the U.S. banking system going to crash?* He then proceeds to answer his question: *I can sum it up in three words. Watch the derivatives* (Snyder, 2014a).

American economist John Exter was very concerned about the astronomical levels of global debt. He is known for creating **Exter's Pyramid** for visualizing the organization of asset classes in terms of risk and size. In Figure 3.1, you will find Exter's Pyramid updated and adapted to illustrate a "conservative" estimate of the value of outstanding derivatives contracts. This global derivatives bubble is estimated to be between $1,500 TRILLION and $1,600 TRILLION dollars. So you see from Figure 3.1 that they don't call it a *pyramid scheme* for nothing. (Durden, 2009), (Durden, 2015a), (Lendman, 2015), (Mayer, 2008), (Snoopman, 2015), (Statista, 2016a), (Statista, 2016b), (U.S. National Debt Clock, 2016) and (Xie, 2015)

< 32 >

Figure 3.1: Exter's Pyramid: The $1,500 TRILLION Dollar Derivatives Bubble

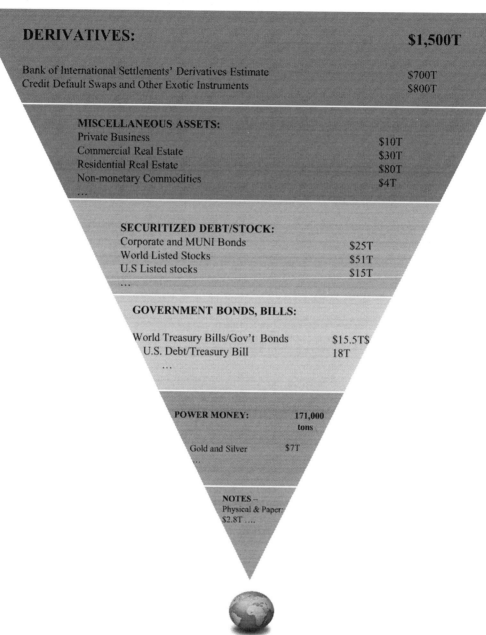

DERIVATIVES: $1,500T

Bank of International Settlements' Derivatives Estimate — $700T
Credit Default Swaps and Other Exotic Instruments — $800T

MISCELLANEOUS ASSETS:
Private Business — $10T
Commercial Real Estate — $30T
Residential Real Estate — $80T
Non-monetary Commodities — $4T
...

SECURITIZED DEBT/STOCK:
Corporate and MUNI Bonds — $25T
World Listed Stocks — $51T
U.S Listed stocks — $15T
...

GOVERNMENT BONDS, BILLS:

World Treasury Bills/Gov't Bonds — $15.5T$
U.S. Debt/Treasury Bill — 18T
...

POWER MONEY: 171,000 tons

Gold and Silver — $7T
...

NOTES –
Physical & Paper:
$2.8T ....

2016 WORLD GDP: Approximately $74 TRILLION

< 33 >

Even more worrisome is the fact that the top five U.S. banks have trillions of dollars in derivatives exposure on their balance sheets – as detailed in Table 3.1. (Snyder 2014b), (Snyder, 2015) and (Durden 2015b)

Table 3.1: *Derivatives Exposure of Top Five U.S. Banks*

	Total Assets	Total Exposure to Derivatives
JP Morgan Chase	$2.6 Trillion	$63 Trillion
Citibank	$1.8 Trillion	$59 Trillion
Goldman Sachs	Less Than $1 Trillion	$57 Trillion
Bank of America	$2.1 Trillion	$54 Trillion
Morgan Stanley	Less Than $1 Trillion	$38 Trillion

3.3 BAIL-OUTS VS. BAIL-INS

The derivatives pyramid is collapsing. Our banks cannot sustain this type of debt, and, frankly, are unsafe. Judging from the derivatives exposure data in Table 3.1 one can draw the conclusion that our banking system is bankrupt. It appears that the American taxpayers are providing last-resort support for risky assets at these insolvent FDIC-insured banks. (FDIC.gov)

Once the derivatives pyramid collapses, these Wall Street banks will need to have some form of bailout. Make no mistake about it, Main Street will be doing these bailouts—AGAIN. To disguise any future "bailouts," new regulations are in place to ensure that Main Street *bails in* these Wall Street banks. (Carter, 2014), (Christenson, 2016), (Durden, 2015b) and (Kuepper, 2016)

❖ *Bail-outs* occur when outside investors (e.g., the U.S. taxpayers) rescue a borrower by injecting money to help meet debt payments. We discussed various bank bail-outs in great detail in Chapter 2.

❖ *Bail-ins* occur when the borrower's creditors are forced to bear some of the burden by having a part of their debt written off. Bail-ins are a way to recapitalize the insolvent banks from within.

< 34 >

Example of a Bank Bail-in: On March 16, 2013, Cyprus announced the terms of its bank bail-in:

- 6.75% confiscation of bank accounts under €100,000 (100,000 Euros)
- 9.9% confiscation of bank accounts larger than €100,000
- A bank holiday is announced.

This bail-in strategy was implemented to eliminate some of the risk for taxpayers by forcing bank customers to share in the pain and suffering (Kuepper, 2016) and (Durden, 2015c).

The bail-outs and the bail-ins are designed to keep the Wall Street banks afloat—at the taxpayers' and/or depositors' expense, respectively. Not many depositors realize that the banks legally own their deposits as soon as they are put in the bank. Your money becomes the bank's, and you essentially become an unsecured creditor holding IOUs or promises to pay. In the case of a bail-in, your IOUs will be converted into "bank equity." With any luck, you will be able to sell your bank stock to someone else in the future for a "decent" price (Bernstein, 2013).

3.4 CHAPTER WRAP-UP

In this chapter, we introduced

- ❖ The benefits and risks of the covered call options strategy—a specific class of financial derivatives
- ❖ The concept of financial derivatives
- ❖ The global significance of the $1,500 TRILLION derivatives bubble
- ❖ Wall Street bail-ins

Armed with this information about the derivatives markets, let us now focus on a specific category of derivatives—the covered call options strategy—to discuss how Main Street can receive a bit of a bailout from Wall Street bankers.

< 35 >

REFERENCES

Bernstein, Leandra, "Dodd-Frank Kills: How the U.S. Joined The International Bail-In Regime." *Larouche Pac,* https://larouchepac.com/052613/bail-dodd-frank-kills, 2014.

Carter, Zach, "Wall Street Demands Derivatives Deregulation In Government Shutdown Bill." *Huffington Post,* http://www.huffingtonpost.com/2014/12/04/wall-street-government-shutdown_n_6272776.html, 2015.

Christenson, Gary, "The FDIC Can No Longer Ensure the Return of Your Deposits!" *Investment Watch,* http://investmentwatchblog.com/the-fdic-can-no-longer-ensure-the-return-of-your-deposits/, 2016.

Durden, Tyler, "The Fed's Nemesis: Exter's $2 Quadrillion Of 'Liquidity'." *Zero Hedge,* http://www.zerohedge.com/article/feds-nemesis-exters-2-quadrillion-liquidity, 2009.

Durden, Tyler, "Gold, The Fed, Exter's Pyramid – When John Exter Met Paul Volcker." *Zero Hedge,* http://www.zerohedge.com/news/2015-08-13/gold-fed-exter's-pyramid---when-john-exter-met-paul-volcker, 2015a.

Durden, Tyler, "Just When You Thought Wall Street's Heist Couldn't Get Any Crazier..." *Zero Hedge,* http://www.zerohedge.com/news/2015-10-25/just-when-you-thought-wall-streets-heist-couldnt-get-any-crazier, 2015b.

Durden, Tyler, "We've All Been Warned (the Cyprus "Bail-In" Model is coming to a Country Near You)." *Zero Hedge,* http://www.zerohedge.com/news/2015-10-28/weve-all-been-warned-cyprus-bail-model-coming-country-near-you, 2015c.

FDIC.gov, *Federal Deposit Insurance Corporation,* https://www.fdic.gov.

Kuepper, Justin, "What Is A Bail-In and How Does It Work?" *International Invest,* http://internationalinvest.about.com/od/glossary/a/What-Is-A-Bail-in-and-How-Does-It-Work.htm, 2016.

Lendman, Stephen, *Global Derivatives: $1.5 Quadrillion Time Bomb,* http://www.globalresearch.ca/global-derivatives-1-5-quadrillion-time-bomb/5464666, 2015.

Mack, Iris Marie, *Energy Trading and Risk Management: A Practical Approach to Hedging, Trading and Portfolio Diversification,* Wiley Finance, Singapore, 2014.

< 36 >

Mayer, Trace, J.D., *The Great Credit Contraction,* http://www.howtovanish.com/products-2/sales/42886/TGCC.pdf, 2008.

Snoopman News, *The Great Financial Wrecking Ball: How Western banks plan to confiscate savers' deposits,* http://snoopman.net.nz/2015/10/26/the-great-financial-wrecking-ball-how-western-banks-plan-to-confiscate-savers-deposits/, 2015.

Snyder, Michael, "The U.S. National Debt Has Grown By More Than A Trillion Dollars In The Last 12 Months." *The Economic Collapse,* http://theeconomiccollapseblog.com/archives/the-u-s-national-debt-has-grown-by-more-than-a-trillion-dollars-in-the-last-12-months, 2014a.

Snyder, Michael, "The six too big to fail banks in the U.S. have 278 trillion dollars of exposure to derivatives." http://theeconomiccollapseblog.com/archives/the-six-too-big-to-fail-banks-in-the-u-s-have-278-trillion-dollars-of-exposure-to-derivatives, 2015.

Snyder, Michael, "5 U.S. Banks Each Have $40,000,000,000,000 In Exposure To Derivatives." *The Trading Report,* http://www.thetradingreport.com/2014/09/25/5-u-s-banks-each-have-40000000000000-in-exposure-to-derivatives/, 2014b.

Statista: The Statistics Portal, "Global GDP (gross domestic product) at current prices from 2010 to 2020 (in billion U.S. dollars)." https://www.statista.com/statistics/268750/global-gross-domestic-product-gdp/, 2016a.

Statista: The Statistics Portal, "Public debt of the United States from 1990 to 2016* (in billion U.S. dollars)." https://www.statista.com/statistics/187867/public-debt-of-the-united-states-since-1990/, 2016b.

U.S. National Debt Clock: Real Time., http://www.usdebtclock.org, 2016.

Wilmott, Paul, Derivatives: *The Theory and Practice of Financial Engineering, Wiley Frontiers in Finance Series,* Singapore, 1998.

Xie, Ye and Andrea Wong, "Once Over $12 Trillion, the World's Currency Reserves Are Now Shrinking." *Bloomberg,* http://www.bloomberg.com/news/articles/2015-04-05/once-over-12-trillion-the-world-s-reserves-are-now-shrinking, 2015.

< 37 >

CHAPTER 4

STOCK OPTIONS

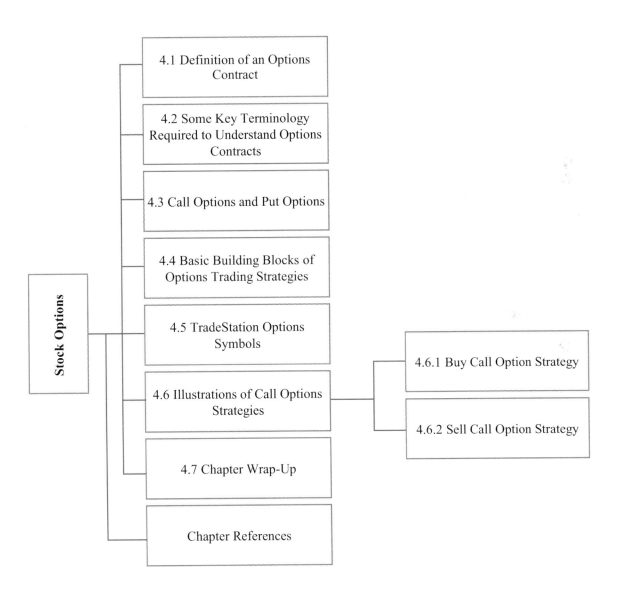

< 38 >

CHAPTER 4

STOCK OPTIONS

In Chapter 3, we introduced and discussed derivatives contracts. There are several different types of derivatives contracts: options, futures, swaps, etc. The type of derivatives contracts we will focus on in this book is the **options contract**.

4.1 DEFINITION OF AN OPTIONS CONTRACT

Options Contract

Definition: An **options contract** is a financial derivatives contract sold by one party (*option writer*) to another party (*option holder*). The options contract offers the option holder the right, but not the obligation, to buy or sell an underlying asset at an agreed-upon price during a certain period or on a specific date.

Note: Depending on the type of options contract, this period could be days, weeks, months, or even a couple of years.

Generally speaking, options may be written on many different types of underlying assets, such as stocks, commodities, foreign currencies, even real estate. In the remainder of our book, we will focus only on **stock options**—that is, options contracts whose underlying assets are stocks (OCC, 1994; OIC, 2016). With stock options, it is possible for investors to

❖ Profit whether a stock's price goes up, down, or remains flat
❖ Cut losses
❖ Protect gains
❖ Control a large number of shares of stocks with a relatively small cash outlay

< 39 >

However, please note that stock options are relatively complex and may be riskier than some other financial assets. Depending on the type of stock options contract bought or sold, an investor may lose his/her entire investment. Why? Because, some options strategies may theoretically expose an investor to unlimited losses. To help you avoid such catastrophic losses and to manage your trading risks, we will systematically define and display various technical terms, trading strategies, case studies, examples, trading charts, graphs, and illustrations to help you make calculated risks when trading stock options. Further discussion of the risks and benefits of stock options will be presented in Chapter 7.

4.2 SOME KEY TERMINOLOGY REQUIRED TO UNDERSTAND OPTIONS CONTRACTS

One needs to understand some new terminology in order to trade stock options. In this section, we will introduce a few key options concepts to get you off on a solid start. These key concepts will be illustrated with TradeStation trading symbols, real market data, and trading charts in Sections 4.5 and 4.6. (Investopedia.com)

Exercise

Exercise: When the options holder invokes the right embedded in the options contract, this is known as "exercising" the options contract.

Strike Price

Strike Price: The strike price is the pre-agreed price per share at which the stock may be purchased or sold by the option holder upon exercise of the options contract. The strike price is also known as the "exercise" price.

Expiration Date

Expiration Date: An expiration date in an options contract is the last day that an options contract is valid. Options may be classified into two groups with respect to the expiration date - European options and American options:

< 40 >

European options

American options

❖ *European options* can be exercised only on the expiration date.
❖ *American options* can be exercised anytime during the life of the options contract. Most of the exchange-traded options are American options.

Premium

Premium

❖ Price **paid** by the options buyer for the options contract. The premium is paid to the seller of the options contract. It is quoted on a per-share basis. The options premium is non-refundable.
❖ Income **received** by the options writer for the options contract sold.

Long

Short

Long versus Short

❖ "Long" implies ownership of a financial asset. For example, if you buy a stock, then you are long that stock in your investment portfolio.
❖ "Short" implies that you have sold a financial asset without actually owning it. I know this seems odd and may take a minute to wrap your brain around, but yes, in the financial markets, you can actually sell something without owning it! However, if you do undertake such a risky trade, you may be obligated to deliver something or to perform a duty at a later date, depending upon the financial asset involved and/or upon the terms of the financial contract.

Open Positions

Closed Positions

Open and Closed Positions

❖ An *open position* is a trade that has been established, or entered into, that has yet to be closed with an opposing trade. For example, an open position can exist following a buy (long) position, or a sell (short) position. In each case, the position will remain open until an opposing trade is made.
❖ A *closed position* is the result of the execution of a transaction that is the exact opposite of an open position, hence nullifying it and eliminating the initial exposure. Closing a long position in a security entails selling it. On the other hand, closing a short position in a security involves buying it back.

< 41 >

Bullish

Bearish

Bullish versus Bearish
- ❖ Investors who believe that the price of a financial asset will increase over time are said to be *bullish.*
- ❖ Investors who believe that the price of a financial asset will decline are said to be *bearish*.

4.3 CALL OPTIONS AND PUT OPTIONS

For each call options contract an investor purchases, he/she has the right (but not the obligation) to purchase 100 shares of a stock at a specific price within a specific time frame.

There are two basic types of stock options: *call options* and *put options*. We present the definitions of these two types of options in Table 4.1.

Table 4.1: *Definition of Calls and Puts*

Call options (aka "calls")	*Put options* (aka "puts")
For each call options contract an investor purchases, he/she has the right (but not the obligation) to purchase 100 shares of a stock at a specific price within a specific time frame.	For each put options contract an investor purchases, he/she has the right (but not the obligation) to sell 100 shares of a stock at a specific price within a specific time frame.
In essence, the investor has the right to "call" stock away from someone.	In essence, the investor has the right to "put" stock to someone.

For each put options contract an investor purchases, he/she has the right (but not the obligation) to sell 100 shares of a stock at a specific price within a specific time frame.

In both the case of calls and puts, the buyer (options holder) has freedom to decide whether or not to exercise the options contract. In addition, the seller (options writer) of the options contract has the obligation to fulfill that right. Of course, the buyer of the options contract will exercise it if it benefits him/her. As illustrated in examples in Section 4.6, such benefits are determined by market conditions, the price of the underlying stock and the terms of the options contract.

< 42 >

4.4 BASIC BUILDING BLOCKS OF OPTIONS TRADING STRATEGIES

Understanding the basic stock options strategies and knowing which strategies to use under different market conditions and outlooks is important for long-term options trading success. The **four basic building blocks of all options strategies** are:

1. *Buy Call*
2. *Buy Put*
3. *Sell (Write) Call*
4. *Sell (Write) Put*

Every options strategy is made up of one or more of these four basic options positions (a.k.a. *options legs*). These four options positions can be combined into many spread positions that can take advantage of almost any market situation:

- ❖ Rising markets
- ❖ Falling markets
- ❖ Quiet markets
- ❖ Rising volatility
- ❖ Falling volatility
- ❖ Other market situations…

In addition, these four options positions also offer unique ways of managing and limiting risk. We will focus on two of these building blocks in this book: buying and selling call options. In Table 4.2, we detail the difference between buying and selling call options.

< 43 >

Table 4.2: *Buy Call and Sell Call Strategies*

Options Strategy	Buy Call	Sell (Write) Call
Definition	The call option buyer has a right, but not the obligation, to buy a specified number of shares of the underlying stock at a fixed price on or before a specific date.	The call option seller (writer) has the obligation to sell a specified number of shares of the underlying stock at a fixed price on or before a specific date. There are two general types of option selling (writing) strategies: *Covered Call*: This type of options selling occurs when the options writer already owns the underlying shares of stocks and wants to make some extra money from these shares. *Naked Call*: This type of options selling occurs when the options seller does not own the underlying shares of stocks. Writing naked calls is a very risky strategy and is not suitable for most novice traders because the seller is still obligated to produce the specified number of shares of the underlying stocks of the options contract.
Right vs. Obligation	The buyer of an option has the right to take action.	The seller (writer) of an option has the obligation to perform a duty.
Bullish versus Bearish	The call buyer is bullish on the underlying stock. Hence, the buyer benefits from an increase in the price of the underlying stock.	The call seller is bearish on the underlying stock. Hence, the seller benefits from a decrease in the price of the underlying stock.
Potential Profit	Unlimited	Limited to the amount collected in options premium
Options Premium	Paid	Received
Risks	Limited to the premium paid for the call options contract	Unlimited in the case of writing naked call options contracts

< 44 >

A *Buy Call* is one of the strategies with which most traders begin trading options. Buying calls can be used as an alternative to the outright purchase of the underlying shares of a stock, with the benefits of limited risk and increased leverage. On the other hand, a *Write Call* is a strategy that most traders use in combination with other options or the underlying stock to create spreads or *Covered Call strategies*. In section 4.6, we will illustrate *Buy Call* and naked *Write Call* strategies. We will further elaborate on the *Covered Call* strategy in subsequent chapters of this book.

4.5 TRADESTATION OPTIONS SYMBOLS

We very much appreciate that *TradeStation, Inc.* allowed us to use their trading platform to illustrate trading strategies in our book. In Figures 4.1 and 4.2, we present the notation for **TradeStation options symbols**. (www.TradeStation.com)

Figure 4.1: **Components of a TradeStation Options Symbol**

The TradeStation options symbols consist of

- ❖ An underlying symbol root
- ❖ Followed by a 2-digit expiration year
- ❖ Followed by a 2-digit expiration month
- ❖ Followed by a 2-digit expiration day
- ❖ Followed by one character (either C or P) indicating the option type (Call or Put)
- ❖ Followed by the strike price
- ❖ Followed by an optional regional exchange designation.

Figure 4.2: **Format of TradeStation Options Symbols**

Format of TradeStation Options Symbols

Composite Symbol Attributes	Composite Symbol
XYZ Corp., 7/20/2016 expiration, $30 Call	XYZ 160720C30
XYZ Corp., 7/20/2016 expiration, $29 Put	XYZ 160720P29

Regional Symbol Attributes	Regional Symbol
XYZ Corp., 7/20/2016 expiration, $30 Call, CBOE	XYZ 160720C30-CO
XYZ Corp., 7/20/2016 expiration, $29 Put, AMEX	XYZ 160720P29-AM

< 45 >

Now using the TradeStation options symbology, let's look at a specific example of a call options symbol whose underlying asset is the stock of Alibaba Group Holding Limited (NYSE:BABA). (Figure 4.3)

Figure 4.3: **Specific example of a call option whose underlying asset is the stock of Alibaba Group Holding Limited (NYSE: BABA)**

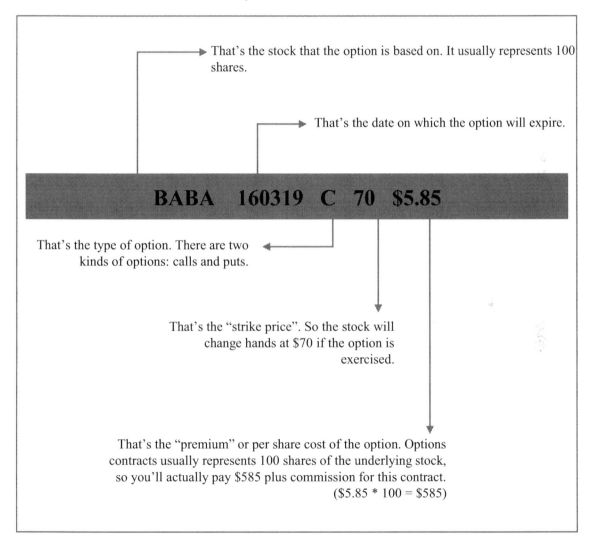

That's the stock that the option is based on. It usually represents 100 shares.

That's the date on which the option will expire.

BABA   160319   C   70 $5.85

That's the type of option. There are two kinds of options: calls and puts.

That's the "strike price". So the stock will change hands at $70 if the option is exercised.

That's the "premium" or per share cost of the option. Options contracts usually represents 100 shares of the underlying stock, so you'll actually pay $585 plus commission for this contract. ($5.85 * 100 = $585)

< 46 >

4.6 ILLUSTRATIONS OF CALL OPTIONS STRATEGIES

4.6.1 *BUY CALL* OPTION STRATEGY

Suppose an investor thinks that Alibaba stock price will increase. In other words, she is "bullish" on BABA. Currently, the price of Alibaba stock is $69.83. The investor's fundamental analysis of Alibaba leads her to believe that its value is higher than its current price. Hence, she decides that she will purchase 500 shares of Alibaba for her investment portfolio.

The investor decides to buy 5 call options contracts with expiration date at March 19th (Table 4.3). These call options can grant her the right (but not the obligation) to buy 500 shares of Alibaba at $70 per share on any given day up until and including March 19th. Please note that this is an American options contract as defined in Section 4.2. It is represented by the TradeStation options symbol **BABA 160319C70.**

The investor paid a premium of $5.85/share for this right - as depicted in Table 4.3. In other words, she bet that the stock price will go up and she paid $500 \times \$5.85 = \$2,925$ plus commission fees for this bet. Note that had the investor purchased 500 shares of Alibaba stock as opposed to the 5 call options contracts, then her initial cash outlay would have been $34,915 plus commission fees.

< 47 >

Table 4.3: *Buy Call Option Strategy – (underlying stock is Alibaba)* **(TradeStation.com)**

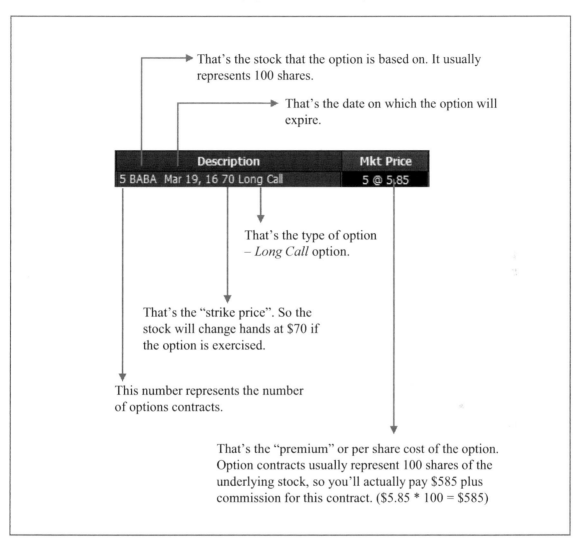

That's the stock that the option is based on. It usually represents 100 shares.

That's the date on which the option will expire.

Description	Mkt Price
5 BABA Mar 19, 16 70 Long Call	5 @ 5.85

That's the type of option – *Long Call* option.

That's the "strike price". So the stock will change hands at $70 if the option is exercised.

This number represents the number of options contracts.

That's the "premium" or per share cost of the option. Option contracts usually represent 100 shares of the underlying stock, so you'll actually pay $585 plus commission for this contract. ($5.85 * 100 = $585)

Now let's analyze the following three scenarios in Table 4.4 to gain a bit of intuition about this buy call options strategy where the underlying is BABA stock.

< 48 >

Table 4.4: *Scenarios of BABA stock prices with respect to the buy call options strategy*

Scenario #1	Scenario #2	Scenario #3
BABA drops below $70 per share	BABA is between $70 and $75.85 per share	BABA is higher than $75.85 per share
In this scenario, the call options contract can be viewed as an "insurance" policy. As we stated above, had the investor bought the 500 shares of BABA instead of the 5 options contracts, she would have paid $34,915 plus commission versus $2,925 plus commission. If there was a large drop in the BABA stock price, then the investor could have lost a substantial amount of money – perhaps much more than the $2,925 plus commissions paid for the 5 call options contract. Having bought the 5 call options contracts instead, she only loses the options premium paid.	The investor will still lose money if she exercises these 5 call options. Why? Because she paid $5.85/share for them. Hence, she only begins to make money if the price of a share of Alibaba's stock is higher than $75.85/share. To use options terminology, this $75.85 is referred to as the **breakeven point** for her options position. Please note that the breakeven point is defined as the market price that a stock must reach for an option buyer to avoid a loss if they exercise the option. For a call buyer, the breakeven point is the strike price plus the premium paid. (Investopedia.com)	Now, we're talking! The investor will finally start to make a profit when BABA is higher than $75.85 plus commissions. The higher the price of BABA, the more she stands to gain from buying the 5 call options contracts.

< 49 >

We can graphically depict these three scenarios in a TradeStation payoff (profit and loss) diagram, as illustrated in Figure 4.4. This payoff diagram is a visual representation of the possible profit and loss of the "buy call" options strategy at a given point in time. To create this payoff diagram, the following data is plotted along the horizontal and vertical axes, respectively.

❖ The values plotted along the horizontal axis (x-axis) represent the Alibaba stock prices – labelled in order with the lower prices on the left and increasing prices towards the right.

❖ The values plotted along the vertical axis (y-axis) represent the potential profit and loss for the Alibaba stock position.

Figure 4.4: **Payoff diagram for Long Call Option on Alibaba (TradeStation.com)**

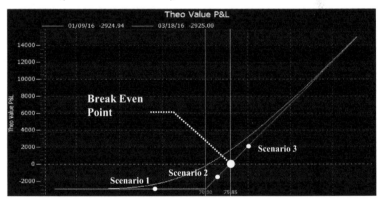

4.6.2 SELL CALL OPTIONS STRATEGY

Now suppose an investor thinks that Alibaba stock price will decline. In other words, he is "bearish" on BABA. Selling (writing) a naked call option on BABA, is also a bearish strategy. Recall we stated in Table 4.2 that this type of options selling occurs when the investor does not own the underlying shares of stocks. However, in this case, the investor is a pretty savvy trader and he decides to short 5 Alibaba call options with expiration date at March 19th. Hence, on any given day up until and including March 19th, he has the obligation to sell 500 shares of Alibaba at $70 per share. In return, he immediately receives the options premiums as a result. In this case, his account is immediately credited $5.85 × 500 = $2,925 (Table 4.5).

< 50 >

Table 4.5: *Short Call Option Strategy – (underlying stock is Alibaba)* **(www.TradeStation.com)**

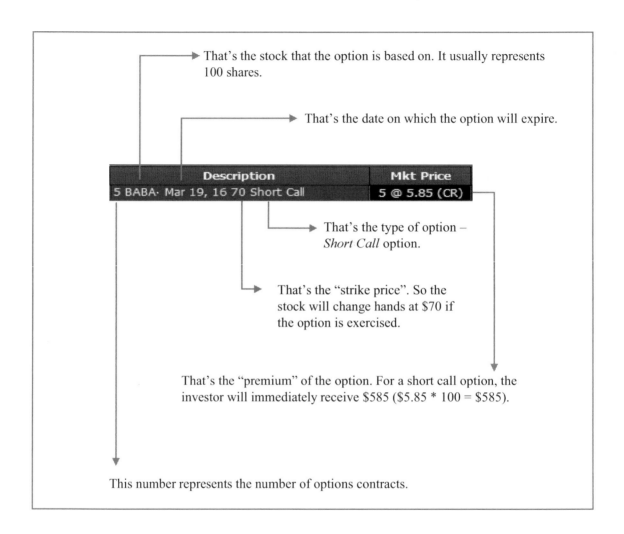

As we did in the previous section, let's analyze the following three scenarios in Table 4.6 to gain a bit of intuition about this sell call options strategy.

< 51 >

Table 4.6: *Scenarios of BABA stock prices with respect to the sell call options strategy*

Scenario #1	Scenario #2	Scenario #3
BABA drops below $70 per share	BABA is between $70 and $75.85 per share	BABA is higher than $75.85 per share
The options contract is worthless to the buyer and will not be exercised. Hence, the options writer gets to keep the $2,925 premium paid.	The options contract is worthless to the buyer and will not be exercised. Hence, the options writer gets to keep the $2,925 premium paid.	The options contract is now valuable to the buyer and he/she will exercise it. Recall, that the options seller does not own the 500 shares because he entered into a naked call options contract. So he is theoretically exposed to unlimited losses – as depicted in Figure 4.5.

This investor will have to go into the market and buy 500 shares of Alibaba stock and turn around and sell these 500 shares of Alibaba stock for $70 per shares.

However, if the investor forecasts a large increase in the price of Alibaba stock, he may wish to consider closing out his naked call options position. |

We can graphically depict these three scenarios in a TradeStation payoff (profit and loss) diagram – as illustrated in Figure 4.5.

< 52 >

Figure 4.5: **Payoff diagram for Short Call Option on Alibaba (www.TradeStation.com)**

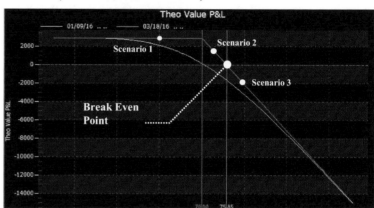

4.7 CHAPTER WRAP-UP

In this chapter, we introduced the following new concepts:

- ❖ Options contracts
- ❖ Stock options
- ❖ Options terminology: exercise, strike price, expiration date, premium, long versus short, American options, European options, breakeven point
- ❖ Open Position versus Closed Positions
- ❖ Bullish versus Bearish
- ❖ Calls and Puts
- ❖ Basic building blocks of options trading strategies: buy call, buy put, sell (write) call, sell (write) put
- ❖ Naked Calls versus Covered Calls
- ❖ TradeStation options symbols
- ❖ Illustrations of call options strategies: buy call, sell (naked) call
- ❖ Payoff (profit and loss) diagrams

Please recall that in the introduction to Chapter 3, we presented a dialogue between one of my former MBA students, Arjun, and a teenager. Arjun told the teenager about the benefits and risks of writing covered call options. Hopefully, what we have presented in this chapter will help you build a solid foundation on options trading strategies and will now allow you to master the covered call strategy, which we will cover in great detail in subsequent chapters. This, my friends, will be your bulletproof trade to help you get paid ---- *Wall Street bailouts for Main Street!!*

< 53 >

REFERENCES

Options Clearing Corporation (OCC), *Characteristics and Risks of Standardized Options*, http://www.optionsclearing.com/components/docs/riskstoc.pdf, 1994.

Options Industry Council (OIC), *Options Education Program*, http://www.optionseducation.org/en.html, 2016.

Investopedia, www.Investopedia.com

TradeStation, www.TradeStation.com

< 54 >

CHAPTER 5

OPTIONS MONEYNESS

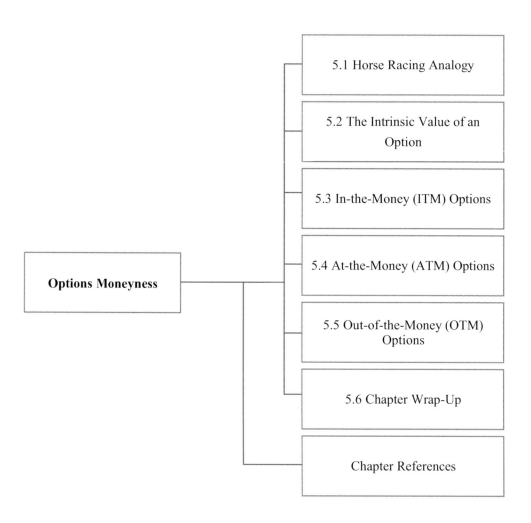

Options Moneyness

- 5.1 Horse Racing Analogy
- 5.2 The Intrinsic Value of an Option
- 5.3 In-the-Money (ITM) Options
- 5.4 At-the-Money (ATM) Options
- 5.5 Out-of-the-Money (OTM) Options
- 5.6 Chapter Wrap-Up
- Chapter References

< 55 >

CHAPTER 5

OPTIONS *MONEYNESS*

In this chapter, we will discuss the concept of the "moneyness" of options. Essentially, moneyness tells option holders whether exercising options will generate a profit.

Moneyness

> **Definition:** *Moneyness* is the relative position of the current price (or future price) of an underlying asset with respect to the strike price of a derivatives contract.

In subsequent sections of this chapter, we will discuss and illustrate the three categories of moneyness:
- ❖ *In-the-Money* (ITM)
- ❖ *At-the-Money* (ATM)
- ❖ *Out-of-the-Money* (OTM)

To help the readers understand these three classifications of moneyness, we will examine a few similarities between options trading and horse racing.

5.1 HORSE RACING ANALOGY

The *World Federation of Exchanges* provides a detailed list of global exchanges for trading options and other financial assets (World-exchanges.org). In one sense, these options exchanges are similar to horse racetracks. At racetracks, there are some who are interested in buying and selling horses. However, many people who frequent racetracks are there to simply bet on the horse races (Investopedia.com).

Let's consider the following analogy in the horse racing business (Benklifa, 2011).

> **Example:** You bet that a horse *Chestnut* will win the next race. Therefore, you spend $10 to bet on *Chestnut*. The four-lap race will begin and you need to wait to see the result at the end. Now suppose you can buy or sell your bet during the race.

< 56 >

After the first lap, your horse is in the lead! If *Chestnut* keeps leading, your lovely horse will bring you a big fortune! Should you sell your bet or keep it? You decide to wait. However, *Chestnut* seems to be tired during the second lap and falls behind now. If you sell your bet you can still get some money back, or you can wait and see. Now *Chestnut* begins speeding in the third lap and keeps leading until the final lap. Unfortunately, your horse *Chestnut* finishes in the fourth place and you get nothing.

This horse race bet is similar to an options trade. Here, you chose not to buy the horse, you simply placed a bet on its outcome in the race. Similarly, you can choose not to buy a stock; you can, instead, decide to buy an option on the stock. What you bet on your horse is similar to what you paid for your option. As previously discussed in Chapter 4, in the options world, we call that amount of money the options *premium.* Your option will expire after a certain period of time (at the end of the race) whether you sell your bet or not. You can win a big fortune if your horse wins that race, but nothing if your lovely horse loses.

5.2 THE *INTRINSIC VALUE* OF AN OPTION

Let's introduce a couple of symbols for a bit of shorthand notation. In addition, we need to define and illustrate the *intrinsic value* of an option to facilitate the explanation of the moneyness of call options.

The market price of the stock is often denoted as "S." In addition, in the options market, the exercise price of an option is often denoted as "K."

> **Example:** For the case of the options written on BABA in Example 4.6.1, we denote K = $70. Hence, this means that the investor has the right, but not the obligation, to buy BABA for $70 from the time the options contract was purchased up until the date the contract expired on March 19, 2016.

< 57 >

In Chapter 4, we introduced the definition of the options *premium* – the price paid by the options buyer for an options contract. As illustrated in Figure 5.1, the options premium consists of two key components – *intrinsic value* and *time value.* Let's examine these components because they will help us understand the moneyness of an option.

Figure 5.1: **Components of the Options Premium**

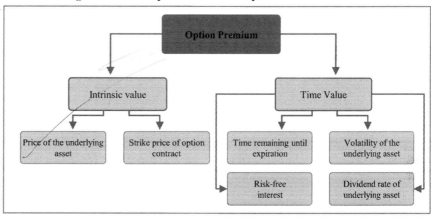

The formal definition of the intrinsic value of an option is as follows:

Intrinsic Value

Definition of *Intrinsic Value*

1. For a call option, the intrinsic value is the difference between the underlying stock's price and the strike price, that is, (S – K).
2. For a put option, the intrinsic value is the difference between the strike price and the underlying stock's price, that is, (K – S).
3. In the case of both puts and calls, if the respective difference value is negative, the intrinsic value is given as zero. The shorthand mathematical notation for this third part of the definition of intrinsic value may be found in Table 5.1. Essentially, it means that the intrinsic value of an option is always positive or zero. It can never be negative.

< 58 >

Table 5.1: *Intrinsic Value and Time Value*

Options Premium = Intrinsic Value + Time Value	
Intrinsic Value	
	Intrinsic Value (Call) = max [S – K, 0]
	Intrinsic Value (Put) = max [K – S, 0]
Time Value	Any premium that is in excess of the option's intrinsic value is referred to as time value.

> *Any premium that is in excess of the option's intrinsic value is referred to as time value.*

We will further elaborate on intrinsic value as we delve into the subsequent sections on ITM, ATM, and OTM. However, before we do that, let's take a look at a simple example of the intrinsic and time value of a call option:

Example: Suppose a call option has a total premium of $9.00. This means that the buyer pays, and the seller receives, $9.00 for each share of stock or $900 for the options contract on 100 shares of stock. If the option has an intrinsic value of $7.00, its time value would be $2.00 per share – calculated as follows:

$$\text{Time Value} = \text{Premium} - \text{Intrinsic Value}$$
$$= \$9.00 - \$7.00 = \$2.00$$

5.3 IN-THE-MONEY (ITM) OPTIONS

Suppose you were smart or lucky enough to bet on a winning horse at a race track. After the race, you claimed your rewards and hence generated some profits from your bet. Yes! Similarly, if your call option is ITM, this means that if you exercise your option, you can eventually gain some profits! Now let's formally define when a call stock option is *In-the-Money:*

< 59 >

In-the-Money

Definition: A call stock option is *In-the-Money* when the strike (exercise) price is lower than the market price of the stock.

In the previous chapter, we illustrated what happens when the strike (exercise) price is lower than the market price of the stock (Section 4.6.1 and Table 4.4). In that example, an investor bought 5 call option contracts by paying a premium of $2,925 as opposed to initially paying $34,915 for the 500 shares of BABA. Recall that the investor will start to make a profit from exercising these options if BABA goes up to $75.85. The higher the price of BABA, the higher the profit from these 5 call options.

Suppose on the options expiration date of March 19, 2016, the market price of BABA was $80 (that is, S = $80). If so, we essentially have Scenario #3 in Table 4.4. However, recall that the investor bought 5 call stock options with the strike price of $70 several days before (that is, K = $70). Hence, these call options are ITM! The investor has the right (but not the obligation) to exercise her 5 call options. Should she exercise them?

❖ If she hadn't bought these options and was interested in BABA shares, she would have to pay the market price of $80 per share.
❖ However, being the smart woman that she is, she had the foresight and knowledge to purchase 5 call options – that is, she made a bet on the movement of the price of BABA first. So, of course she should exercise these ITM call options. She can then pay $70 to get one BABA share which is worth $80 in the market.

Please see Figure 5.2 below to see what her payoff will be when she exercises the options. Remember we have to factor in the call premium of $5.85 per share when we calculate the options payoff.

< 60 >

Figure 5.2: **Payoff for an ITM call option with a strike price of $70 (per share)**

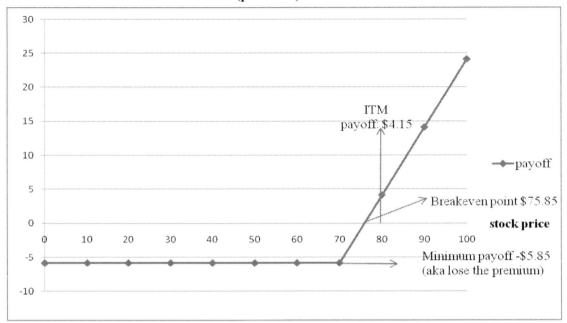

Utilizing the definition of intrinsic value introduced in Section 5.1, let's see if these 5 ITM call options have any intrinsic value on the expiration date. Doing a bit of math, we calculate the intrinsic value as follows:

$$\text{Intrinsic Value} = \max[S-K,\ 0]$$
$$= \max[\$80 - \$70,\ 0] = \max[\$10,0] = \$10 > 0$$

Hence, each of these 5 ITM call options has an intrinsic value of $10 at the time of expiration. Please note that we have not included the brokerage commission (cost of buying the call option) in the previous calculations. This may vary depending on the type of brokerage account an investor has and which brokerage firm he/she uses.

5.4 AT-THE-MONEY (ATM) OPTIONS

Once again, we revisit Table 4.4 in the previous chapter. Suppose that on the options expiration date of March 19, 2016, the market price of BABA equals the strike price. That is, S = K = $70. In this case, the options are said to be *At-the-Money:*

< 61 >

At-the-Money

Definition: A call stock option is *At-the-Money* when the strike (exercise) price and the market price of the stock are equal.

The investor has the right (but not the obligation) to exercise her 5 call options. Should she exercise them?

❖ If she hadn't purchased these options and was interested in BABA shares, she may choose to pay the market price of $70 per share.
❖ However, instead of purchasing the BABA shares, she placed a bet on the movement of the price of BABA by purchasing options on BABA. At first glance, one would think that it makes sense for the investor to exercise these ATM options because S = K. However, remember there is that pesky little thing call "options premium." In this example, the premium is $5.85 per share. So when the stock price is equal to the strike price, exercising the ATM option is not profitable. In this case, the investor should choose to let this ATM option expire.

Please see Figure 5.3 below to see what the investor's payoff will be for these ATM options at the time of expiration.

Figure 5.3: **Payoff for an ATM call option with a strike price of $70 (per share)**

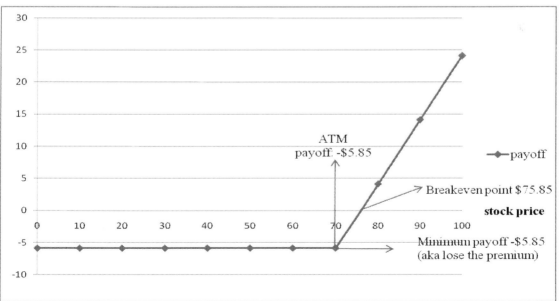

< 62 >

Now let's see if these 5 ATM call options have any intrinsic value on the expiration date. Doing a bit of math, we calculate the intrinsic value as follows:

$$\text{Intrinsic Value} = \max[S\text{-}K, 0]$$
$$= \max[\$70 - \$70, 0] = \max[0,0] = 0$$

Hence, each of these 5 ATM call options has zero intrinsic value at the time of expiration. For an ATM option, the right thing to do is to ignore the option – just let the options contract expire. You will, however, lose the premium you paid upfront for the options contract. Remember, never exercise an ATM option, as it has no intrinsic value. Please note that once again, we have not included the brokerage commissions in these calculations.

5.5 OUT-OF-THE-MONEY (OTM) OPTIONS

Let's go back to our horse racing analogy again. Your horse Chestnut is in the lead after the first lap and you decide not to trade your bet. However, Chestnut falls back into the fourth position in the final lap. Hence, no rational, sober human being will pay a penny for your bet. This losing horse race bet is analogous to Scenario #1 in Table 4.4 of the previous chapter. Suppose on the options expiration date of March 19, 2016, the market price of BABA is less than the strike price? For sake of illustration, we will assume that S = $60 at expiration. In this case, the options are said to be *Out-of-the-Money:*

Out of the Money

Definition: A call stock option is ***Out-of-the-Money*** when the strike (exercise) price is higher than the market price of the stock.

The investor has the right (but not the obligation) to exercise her 5 call options. Should she exercise them?

❖ If she hadn't bought these options and was interested in BABA shares, she may choose to pay the market price of $60 per share for BABA.

< 63 >

❖ Or, if instead of purchasing the BABA stocks, she placed a bet on the movement of the price of BABA by purchasing options on BABA. It makes no financial sense for the investor to exercise these options! If she can buy the same stock at $60, why should she pay $70 instead! So when the strike price is higher than the stock price, the call option will not be exercised.

Please see Figure 5.4 below to see what the investor's payoff will be at the time of expiration.

Figure 5.4: **Payoff for an OTM call option with a strike price of $70 (per share)**

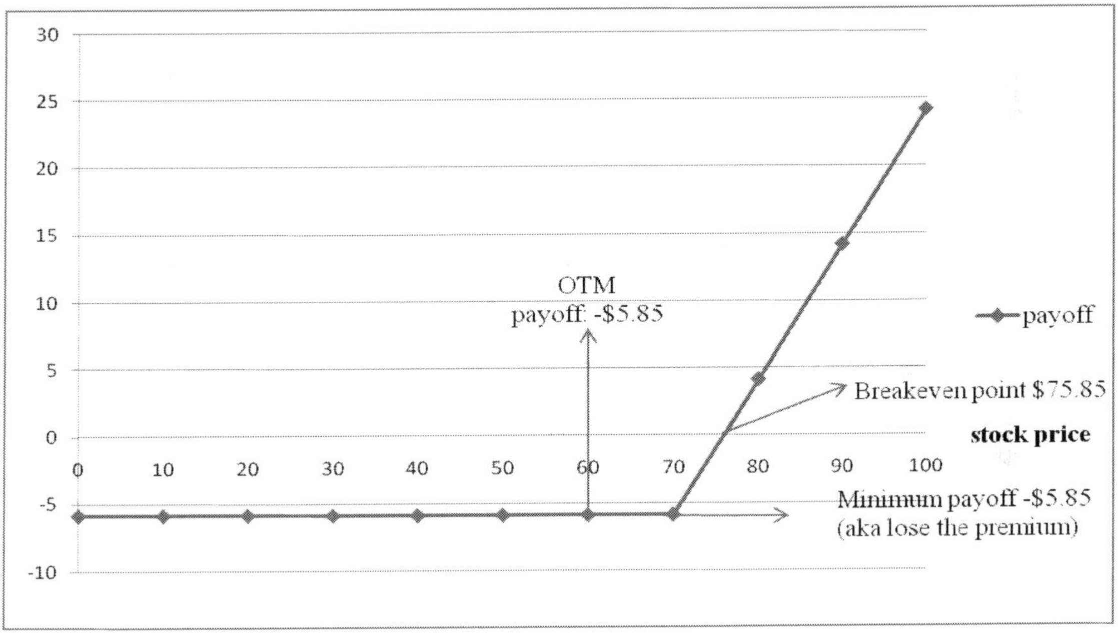

Now let's see if these 5 OTM call options have any intrinsic value on the expiration date. Doing a bit of math, we calculate the intrinsic value as follows:

Intrinsic Value = max[S-K, 0]
= max[$60 - $70, 0] = max[-$10,0] = 0

< 64 >

Hence, each of these 5 OTM call options has zero intrinsic value at the time of expiration. For an OTM option, the right thing to do is to ignore the option – just let the options contract expire. You will, however, lose the premium you paid upfront for the options contract. Remember, never exercise an OTM option, as it has no intrinsic value. Please note that, once again, we have not included the brokerage commissions in these calculations.

5.6 CHAPTER WRAP-UP

In summary, in this chapter we have discussed the moneyness of options and similarities to horse racing – as detailed in Table 5.2:

Table 5.2: *Horse Racing Analogy*

	Horse Race	Options Trade
What you pay upfront	Wager	Premium
Underlying Asset	Horse	Stock
Maturity Date	End of the race	Exercise Date
What determines your payoff?	Your horse rank	Stock price
What is your payoff?	Depends on the rates *(Please see note below and Figure 5.5)*	Depends on the option type and the intrinsic value

Note: In horse racing, we can see the rates (or odds) before betting on horses. Here, rates (odds) mean how much you will get by paying $1 dollar. For example, a horse rated 10-1 (or written as 10/1) means you will earn $10 dollar by betting $1 dollar if you bet the right horse (Form Ratings).

< 65 >

Figure 5.5: Details of Horse Race Ratings

NO	HORSE	AGE	LR*	2LR*	3LR*	9LR*	SPEED	FNSH*	TOTAL*	ODDS FCST*
1	Who Owns Me (IRELAND)	6	105	21	25	182	32	10	224	11/4
2	Lieutenant Miller	6	90	43	20	185	0	8	197	7/2
10	The Good Guy (IRELAND)	9	80	19	21	151	31	9	192	6/1
5	Nez Rouge (FRENCH)	11	60	46	20	155	20	7	185	8/1
3	Oscars Secret (IRELAND)	5	70	35	17	153	0	4	158	8/1
9	Occasionally Yours (IRELAND)	8	61	26	14	128	21	7	157	12/1
4	Phare Isle (IRELAND)	7	44	22	12	119	25	11	156	14/1
8	Go Amwell	9	43	20	13	104	24	6	135	16/1
6	Jive Master (IRELAND)	7	44	26	10	105	0	5	113	10/1
7	Manshoor (IRELAND)	7	49	18	9	100	0	7	106	16/1
LR		Last Run-The horse's rating for its last race.								
2LR		The horse's rating for its last two races.								
3LR		The horse's rating for its last three races.								
9LR		The horse's rating for its last nine races.								
FNSH		Finish-The position of the last race.								
TOTAL		The horse's total score.								
ODDS FCST		Odds forecast.								

With respect to the moneyness of options, we can use the following table (Table 5.3) to help us summarize what we have discussed in this chapter:

< 66 >

Table 5.3: *Moneyness of options at expiration date*

Call Option	Stock Price of BABA (S)	Strike Price (K)	Exercise or not	Intrinsic Value	Formula
In the Money	$80	$70	Yes	$10	S>K
At the Money	$70	$70	No	0	S=K
Out of the Money	$60	$70	No	0	S<K

We summarize the *moneyness* of a long call option in Figure 5.6. To make the moneyness easy to remember, we don't show other factors influencing the payoff, such as commission, in the figure.

Figure 5.6: **Moneyness of a long call option with a strike price of $70 (per share)**

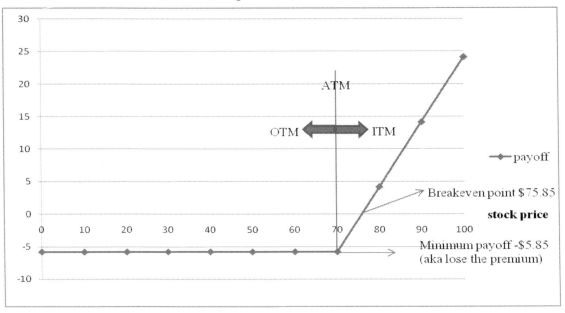

We hope you can see that with a bit of effort and practice, options are relatively easy to grasp. However, don't feel overwhelmed with all the new options terminology. With time, you will feel more comfortable with them. We hope that this chapter helps lay the groundwork for understanding what is going on in the options market. Once you master the information presented in this chapter, you are one step closer to conquer the world of options trading and to get your Main Street bailouts from Wall Street.

< 67 >

REFERENCES

Benklifa, Michael Hanania, *Profiting with Iron Condor Options: Strategies from the Frontline for Trading in Up or Down Markets,* FT Press, 2011.

Form Ratings, *What horse ratings look like,*
http://formratings.co.uk/form-rating-examples/

Investopedia.com, http://www.investopedia.com/terms/i/intrinsicvalue.asp

World-Exchanges.org, *Wfe Members,*
http://www.world-exchanges.org/home/index.php/members/wfe-members

< 68 >

CHAPTER 6

DON'T GET MAD, GET EVEN: WALL STREET BAILOUTS FOR MAIN STREET

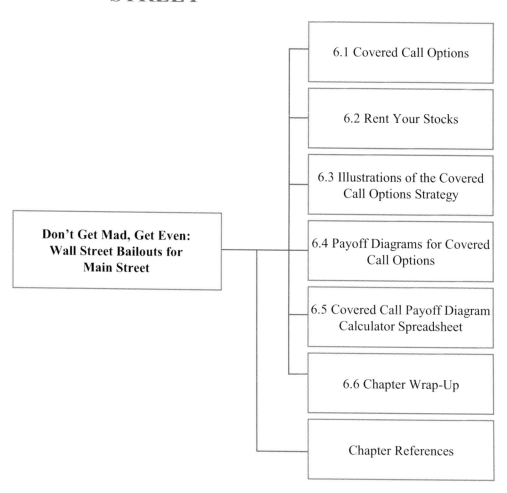

Don't Get Mad, Get Even: Wall Street Bailouts for Main Street

- 6.1 Covered Call Options
- 6.2 Rent Your Stocks
- 6.3 Illustrations of the Covered Call Options Strategy
- 6.4 Payoff Diagrams for Covered Call Options
- 6.5 Covered Call Payoff Diagram Calculator Spreadsheet
- 6.6 Chapter Wrap-Up
- Chapter References

< 69 >

CHAPTER 6

DON'T GET MAD, GET EVEN: WALL STREET BAILOUTS FOR MAIN STREET

Recall, as discussed in Chapter 4 (Table 4.2), there are two general types of option selling (writing) strategies – *naked call* and *covered call.*

> *Naked Call*: This type of options selling occurs when the options seller does not own the underlying shares of stocks. Writing naked calls is a very risky strategy and is not suitable for most novice traders because the seller is still obligated to produce the specified number of shares of the underlying stocks of the options contract.

> *Covered Call*: This type of options selling occurs when the options writer already owns the underlying shares of stocks and wants to make some extra money from these shares.

Also, please recall that in section 4.6, we illustrated the *naked call* strategy. Now, in this chapter, we will utilize the knowledge gained thus far to elaborate on the *covered call* strategy. As discussed in Chapter 3, some of the key benefits and risks of the covered call options strategy were presented in this dialogue between one of my MBA students and a teenager:

> **Arjun:** Hey kid. A covered call options strategy is a great way to make money. Basically, this strategy involves

> ❖ Buying shares of a stock – also known as going long these shares of stock.

> ❖ Simultaneously writing a call option – also known as selling a call option, or shorting a call option.

A covered call options strategy is a great way to make money. Basically, this strategy involves

- *Buying shares of a stock – also known as going long these shares of stock.*
- *Simultaneously writing a call option – also known as selling a call option, or shorting a call option.*

< 70 >

Teenager: What are the benefits and risks of a covered call option strategy?

Arjun: The main benefit of writing a covered call option is that it is an income-generating strategy. Think of it like this: an exchange is paying you money to hold onto a stock that you already own. A covered call strategy will work well if the price of the stock rises slightly or stays the same. While you can have heavy losses from writing covered calls if the price of the stock falls significantly, the maximum gain can also be very high. The maximum gain will basically be the premium collected from writing a call option plus the difference between the "exercise" price and the stock price at expiration.

Building upon the material presented thus far, we now have a solid foundation to master the covered call options strategy. Remember, the covered call strategy will be your bulletproof trade to help you get paid — a *Wall Street bailout for Main Street!*

6.1 COVERED CALL OPTIONS

Now let us discuss *covered call options* – also known as covered/married stock options. (TradeStation) The call is said to be "covered" because the potential obligation to deliver the stock can be satisfied using the stock held in the investor's portfolio. Are covered calls "better" than naked calls? Well, the primary difference between the two types of option is as follows:

❖ Naked call writers sell call options without owning the underlying shares of stocks noted in the options contract. If the stock price increases very much, naked call writers will be forced to buy the stocks for delivery because they did not purchase the underlying shares of stocks that the call option is written on.

< 71 >

❖ Covered call writers sell call options on shares of stocks they already own or plan to purchase at the time of opening the options contract. If the stock price increases very much, covered call writers will not be forced to buy the stocks for delivery because they already purchased the underlying shares of stocks that the call option is written on.

So compared to naked call options, covered call options are less risky to trade. As we will illustrate in subsequent sections of this chapter, the covered call options strategy provides downside protection on the stock while allowing the investor to generate extra revenues. Hence, this is why many novice traders find it relatively straightforward to introduce covered call options into their investment portfolios.

Please recall our naked call option examples from previous chapters – that is, examples of call options written (sold) on BABA even though the investor did not own shares of BABA in her portfolio. Now suppose an investor decides to build a covered call options strategy instead of a naked call strategy on underlying shares of BABA. That is, the investor will sell options on shares of BABA he/she already owns and/or plans to purchase before opening the call options contract.

For sake of comparison with the naked call options examples from Chapter 4, we will assume similar terms for the covered call options examples in this chapter:

❖ BABA is the underlying asset noted in the call options contract.
❖ BABA is trading at $69.83 per share when the call options contract is opened.
❖ The call option has a strike price of $70.
❖ The call option has a premium of $5.85 per share.
❖ The expiration date is March 19, 2016.
❖ The investor decides to write 5 call option contracts on 500 shares of BABA she recently purchased. Recall that one option contract is written on 100 shares.

< 72 >

In summary, the investor's covered call options trading strategy consists of the following positions:

- ❖ Buy 500 shares of BABA – that is, go long 500 shares of BABA.
- ❖ Simultaneously, sell (write) 5 call options on BABA – that is, short 5 call options on BABA.

6.2 RENT YOUR STOCKS

In case you may be wondering why an investor would want to trade a combination of long stock positions and short call options positions, let's consider the following real estate example:

> **Real Estate Rental Analogy**: If you own a rental property but aren't leasing it, you may be leaving money on the table. However, once you lease your property, you can begin to generate extra income! In exchange for the leasing of your property, you will receive rent payments. Similarly, if you own stocks and decide to hold them for a while, you can also "rent your stocks" to generate some extra revenues by writing covered call options on your stocks! In exchange for the rental of your stocks, you will receive the call option premium for the shares of stock rented (Brown, 2016).

Hopefully this simple real estate analogy gives you a bit of intuition as to why savvy investors utilize the covered call options strategy to "rent" their stock to exchanges. There is no need for investors to leave any money on the table. In Section 6.3 we will discuss and illustrate how to rent stock via the covered call options strategy. In addition, in Section 6.4 we present the options payoff diagrams for this stock rental strategy.

< 73 >

6.3 ILLUSTRATIONS OF THE COVERED CALL OPTIONS STRATEGY

As we did in Chapter 4 for the naked call options strategy, let's analyze various scenarios to gain a bit of intuition about the covered call options strategy.

Scenario #1: BABA drops from $69.83 to $63 per share.
So now S=$63 and K is still $70. The option is OTM and has no intrinsic value. No one will exercise this call option and, therefore, the investor can keep the premium and keep the shares of BABA. Recall, the premium is $5.85 per share and the investor shorted 5 call options written on 500 shares. So the total premium the investor will receive is $5.85*500=$2,925. However, the investor will lose some profits from holding the stock: $69.83-$63=$6.83 per share due to the drop in the price of BABA shares. The total loss due to the drop in the price of BABA shares is $6.83*500=$3,415. So the investor's total cash flow is $2,925-$3,415=-$490. Hence, in this case, the investor's covered call options strategy provided some downside protection on the shares of BABA when the price dropped from $69.83 to $63 per share.

Scenario #2: BABA drops from $69.83 to $63.98 per share.
So now we have S=$63.98 and once again K=$70. The option is also OTM and has no intrinsic value. Therefore, this option will not be exercised. But the investor will lose $69.83-$63.98=$5.85 per share because the BABA stock price declined. The total loss for these 500 shares of BABA is $5.85*500=$2,925. As in Scenario #1, the investor receives $2,925 in options premiums. Hence, the investor's total cash flow is $2,925-$2,925=0. Once again, the covered call options strategy provided some downside protection on the investor's shares of BABA when the price dropped from $69.83 to $63.98 per share.

< 74 >

Scenario #3: BABA drops from $69.83 to $68 per share.
So now we have S=$68 and once again K=$70. The option is still OTM and has no intrinsic value. No one will exercise the option and the investor can keep the $2,925 premium. However, the investor will lose $69.83-$68=$1.83 per share. The total cash outflow on the BABA stock holding is $1.83*500=$915. Therefore, the investor's total cash flow is $2,925-$915=$2010. Once again, the covered call strategy provided some downside protection on the shares of BABA when the price dropped from $69.83 to $68 per share. However, thanks to the covered call options strategy, the investor still gains some profits even though the BABA stock price dropped from $69.83 to $68.

Scenario #4: BABA increases from $69.83 to $70 per share.
Now the BABA stock price is the same as the strike price. This call option is ATM, although it has zero intrinsic value. Hence, it will not be exercised. Therefore, the investor can still keep the $2,925 premium. In addition, the investor also gains $70-$69.83=$0.17 per share because she owns the stock. The total cash flow on the BABA stock holding is $0.17*500=$85. Therefore, the investor's total cash flow is $2,925+$85=$3,010.

Scenario #5: BABA increases from $69.83 to $78 per share.
Unfortunately, the investor is on the wrong side of the market when she chose this call option. This call option is ITM and will be exercised. But fortunately, the investor has the shares of BABA stocks in her portfolio. Now she has to sell her BABA stock for $70 per share to option holders even though they are worth $78 per share. So, if the investor bought the shares for $69.83 per share and sold them at $70 per share she will only gain $0.17 for each share. The total cash flow on the BABA stock holding is $85 as we calculated in Scenario 4. In addition, the investor already has had the $2,925 options premium credited to her investment account.

< 75 >

Therefore, the total cash flow is $2,925+$85=$3,010. Note, in such a case where the price of the underlying stock has such a large increase from $69.83 to $78 per share a savvy investor may consider closing this covered call position – as we defined in Chapter 4. In doing so, she will be able to take advantage of the large increase in the BABA stock price.

To help our readers digest these five covered call options scenarios and better understand how the options behave with respect to changes in the underlying stock price, we have compiled all the analyses in Table 6.1.

❖ We can see that when the BABA stock price drops, the premium received from the covered call options strategy provided some downside protection. For instance, in Scenario #3, the BABA stock price dropped but we still made a profit on this trade. More explicitly, the covered call strategy provided downside protection on the stock while allowing the investor to generate extra revenues.

❖ Now if we compare the results of Scenarios #4 and #5 in Table 6.1 to those in Table 4.6, we see that when the stock price increases, covered call writers earn more than naked call writers! However, we also see that the upside gains are capped in the case of the covered call options. That is, the most the investor can make off this strategy is $3,010.00 – regardless as to how much the stock price increases. Note: The only way the investor may take advantage of all the upside gain in the stock price will be to close out the covered call options position.

< 76 >

Table 6.1: *Scenarios of How the Covered Call Options Strategy Changes with Respect to the BABA Stock Prices*

Cash Flow	Scenario #1	Scenario #2	Scenario #3	Scenario #4	Scenario #5
Original Stock Price	$69.83	$69.83	$69.83	$69.83	$69.83
Current Stock Price (S)	$63.00	$63.98	$68.00	$70.00	$78.00
Moneyness	OTM	OTM	OTM	ATM	ITM
Premium	$5.85	$5.85	$5.85	$5.85	$5.85
Strike Price (K)	$70.00	$70.00	$70.00	$70.00	$70.00
Profit: Holding Stocks	($3,415.00)	($2,925.00)	($915.00)	$85.00	$4,085.00
Profit: Exercising Options	$0.00	$0.00	$0.00	$0.00	($4,000.00)
Profit: Premium	$2,925.00	$2,925.00	$2,925.00	$2,925.00	$2,925.00
Total Cash Flow	($490.00)	$0.00	$2,010.00	$3,010.00	$3,010.00

6.4 PAYOFF DIAGRAMS FOR COVERED CALL OPTIONS

As discussed in Section 6.1, the covered call options strategy involves two types of trades: long stocks and short call options. Now we will graphically illustrate the covered call options strategy via the presentations of the following payoff diagrams:

Payoff diagram #1 is for long shares of BABA stocks.

Payoff diagram #2 is for naked short call options where the underlying assets are shares of BABA stocks.

Payoff diagram #3 is for covered call options written on shares of BABA stocks.

Note: We will see that the payoff diagram #3 is a combination of payoff diagrams #1 and #2.

< 77 >

Figure 6.1: **Payoff for holding BABA stock (500 shares)**

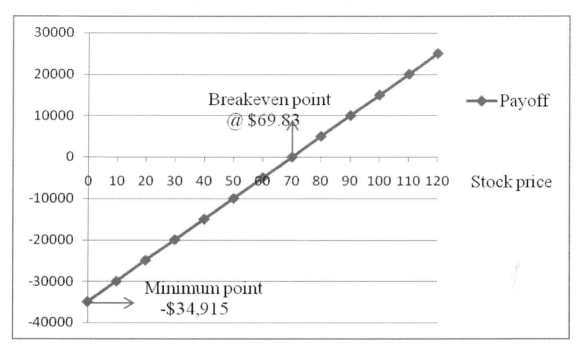

Figure 6.2: **Payoff for shorting call options on BABA stock (5 call options)**

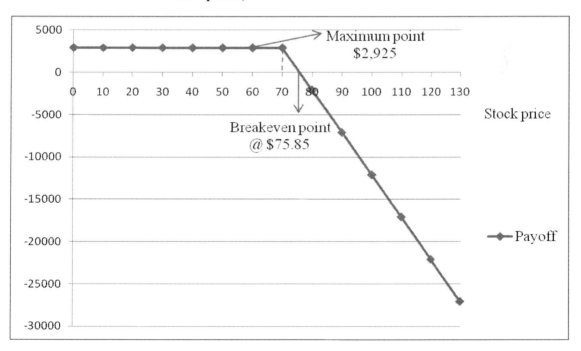

< 78 >

Please recall that our covered call options trade consists of two positions: long 500 shares of BABA stock and short 5 call options. Hence, the payoff diagram for our covered call trade is simply the addition of the graphs in Figure 6.1 and Figure 6.2 - yielding Figure 6.3.

Figure 6.3: **Payoff diagram for writing a covered call option on BABA (500 shares and 5 call options)**

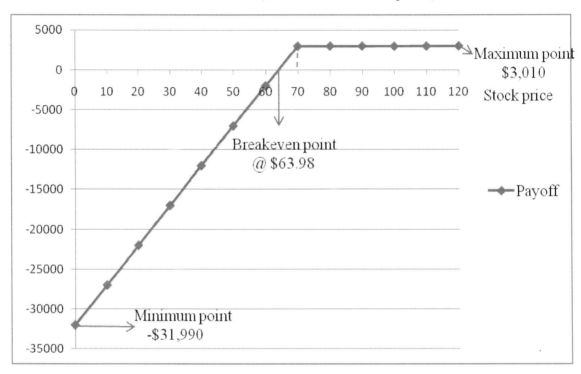

6.5 COVERED CALL PAYOFF DIAGRAM CALCULATOR SPREADSHEET

As can be seen in Figure 6.4, we have developed a covered call option payoff diagram calculator spreadsheet for our readers. It will be made available on our website www.MainStBailout.com. This calculator can help you analyze your covered call options strategies and to graph payoff diagrams. Hopefully, this calculator will help you become a hot shot options trader.

< 79 >

Figure 6.4: **Covered call calculator**

6.6 CHAPTER WRAP-UP

In this chapter, we discussed the following:

❖ How to make money renting your stocks to an exchange by trading covered call options
❖ Five scenarios to illustrate the unique features of the covered call options strategy
❖ How a covered call options strategy gives a trader some downside protection when the stock price drops significantly
❖ How the covered call options strategy helps traders generate some extra revenues when the stock price is relatively flat
❖ A covered call options calculator spreadsheet that may be accessed from our website www.MainStBailout.com (Figure 6.4)
❖ The difference between writing a covered call, a naked call, and holding stocks – as summarized in Table 6.2 below

< 80 >

Table 6.2: *Cash Flow for Covered Calls, Naked Calls, and Long Stocks*

Cash Flow	OTM Option	ATM Option	ITM Option
Original Stock Price	$69.83	$69.83	$69.83
Current Stock Price (S)	$63.00	$69.83	$78.00
Premium	$5.85	$5.85	$5.85
Strike Price (K)	$70.00	$70.00	$70.00
Profit: Holding Stocks	($3,415.00)	$0.00	$4,085.00
Profit: Exercising Options	$0.00	$0.00	($4,000.00)
Profit: Premium	$2,925.00	$2,925.00	$2,925.00
Total Cash Flow: Covered Call Writer	($490.00)	$2,925.00	$3,010.00
Total Cash Flow: Naked Call Writer	$2,925.00	$2,925.00	($1,075.00)
Total Cash Flow: Holding Stocks Only	($3,415.00)	$0.00	$4,085.00

So, from now on, if you find yourselves getting mad over the Wall Street bank bailouts, remember that you don't need to get mad - just get even by trading covered call options to get your Main Street bailout!

< 81 >

REFERENCES

Tradestation, www.tradestation.com

Brown, Thomas, "Rent Your Stock to Riches." *Rapid Profit Formula,* http://rapidprofitformula.net/rent-your-stock-to-riches/, 2016.

< 82 >

CHAPTER 7

COVERED CALLS: BENEFITS, RISKS AND SWOT ANALYSIS

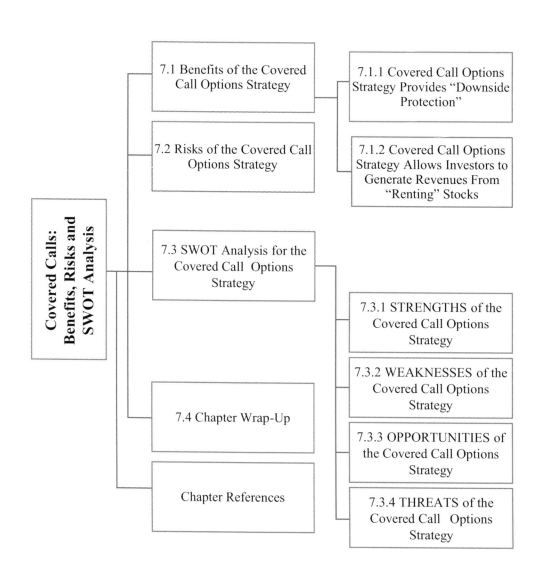

- Covered Calls: Benefits, Risks and SWOT Analysis
  - 7.1 Benefits of the Covered Call Options Strategy
    - 7.1.1 Covered Call Options Strategy Provides "Downside Protection"
    - 7.1.2 Covered Call Options Strategy Allows Investors to Generate Revenues From "Renting" Stocks
  - 7.2 Risks of the Covered Call Options Strategy
  - 7.3 SWOT Analysis for the Covered Call Options Strategy
    - 7.3.1 STRENGTHS of the Covered Call Options Strategy
    - 7.3.2 WEAKNESSES of the Covered Call Options Strategy
    - 7.3.3 OPPORTUNITIES of the Covered Call Options Strategy
    - 7.3.4 THREATS of the Covered Call Options Strategy
  - 7.4 Chapter Wrap-Up
  - Chapter References

< 83 >

CHAPTER 7

COVERED CALLS: BENEFITS, RISKS AND SWOT ANALYSIS

In Chapters 3 through 6, we discussed and illustrated the covered call options strategy. This type of low-risk income-generating strategy is derived based on the assumption that the underlying stock price slightly increases or remains unchanged during the life of the options contract. In this chapter, we highlight the potential benefits and risks of the covered call options strategy. This analysis may be found in Sections 7.1 and 7.2. In addition, in Section 7.3, we present a SWOT analysis of the covered call options strategy - utilized to examine how both external and internal factors affect this type of trading strategy.

7.1 BENEFITS OF THE COVERED CALL OPTIONS STRATEGY

To clearly illustrate and summarize the benefits of the covered call options strategy to our readers and to maintain some consistency with previous chapters, we will assume similar terms for the covered call options examples in this chapter:

- ❖ BABA is the underlying asset noted in the call options contract.
- ❖ BABA is trading at $69.83 per share when the call options contract is opened.
- ❖ The call option has a strike price of $70.
- ❖ The call option has a premium of $5.85 per share.
- ❖ The expiration date is March 19, 2016.
- ❖ The investor decides to write 5 call options contracts on 500 shares of BABA she recently purchased. Recall that one call options contract is written on 100 shares.

< 84 >

In summary, the investor's covered call options trading strategy consists of the following positions:

- ❖ Buy 500 shares of BABA – that is, go long 500 shares of BABA
- ❖ Simultaneously, sell (write) 5 call options on BABA – that, is short 5 call options on BABA

In the previous chapters we presented several payoff diagrams to illustrate profits generated when an investor utilizes the covered call options strategy. To emphasize the various benefits and risks associated with the covered call options strategy, we include the following screenshot (Figure 7.1), displaying the prices of BABA stock from February 10, 2016 to March 30, 2016. Observe that the price of BABA stock was slightly higher than $74.50 per share on the expiration date March 19, 2016.

Figure 7.1: **Stock Prices for Alibaba Group Holding Ltd. (BABA) (Tradestation.com)**

We will utilize this data and options contract terms to illustrate the two most important benefits of the covered call options strategy:

1. Downside Protection
2. Revenues from "Stock Rental"

< 85 >

7.1.1 COVERED CALL OPTIONS STRATEGY PROVIDES "DOWNSIDE PROTECTION"

Please note that in Tables 7.1 through 7.3, we will only illustrate the most significant benefits investors receive when utilizing the covered call options strategy; other benefits will be described in Section 7.3 – where we discuss a SWOT Analysis for covered calls.

As discussed and illustrated in Section 6.3, the covered call options strategy provides some downside protection when the stock price drops. In other words, the covered call options strategy is a way to protect your wealth. Let's consider a scenario where the price of BABA drops from $69.83 to $63 per share. In Table 7.1, we compare the portfolio losses **with** and **without** the implementation of the covered call options strategy.

Table 7.1: *Benefits of Downside Protection*

BABA drops from $69.83 to $63 per share.	
WITHOUT the covered call strategy	Recall that the stock price per share prior to opening the options contract is $69.83. Due to adverse market conditions, the current price of BABA drops to $63. Hence, the total loss for the investor due to this lower stock price is ($69.83-$63)*500=$3,415.
WITH the covered call strategy	Fortunately, the investor is very savvy and decided to sell five covered call options on these 500 shares of BABA stocks before the stock price dropped from $69.83 to $63.
	So now, BABA's price is $63 and the option's strike price is $70. This option is OTM and has no intrinsic value. No one will exercise this option and, therefore, the investor can keep the options premium (worth a total of $5.85*500=$2,925) and keep her shares of BABA.
	In this situation, the investor's total cash flow is $2,925-$3,415= -$490. Compared to the cash flow in the previous *WITHOUT* scenario (-$3,415), this loss of -$490 makes the investor a "happy camper."
	Hence, we see that the covered call options strategy provided the investor some downside protection on the shares of BABA when the price dropped from $69.83 to $63 per share.

< 86 >

7.1.2 COVERED CALL OPTIONS STRATEGY ALLOWS INVESTORS TO GENERATE REVENUES FROM "RENTING" STOCKS

Please recall the real estate analogy presented in Section 6.2 of the previous chapter. If you own stocks and decide to hold them for a while, you can also "rent your stocks" to generate some extra revenues by writing call options on your stocks! In exchange for the rental of your stocks, you will receive the call option premium for the shares of stocks rented. This conservative trading strategy can be more lucrative than just "hoping and praying" that the price of the stock owned will increase.

In Tables 7.2 and 7.3, we illustrate how the covered call options strategy can be utilized to generate additional profits in both bullish and bearish market conditions, respectively.

Table 7.2: *Benefits of "Stock Rental" in Bearish Markets*

BABA drops from $69.83 to $68 per share.	
WITHOUT the covered call strategy	Recall that the stock price per share prior to opening the options contract is $69.83. Due to bearish market conditions, the current price of BABA is now $68. Hence, the total cash outflow on the BABA stock holding is ($69.83-$68)*500=$915.
WITH the covered call strategy	So now, BABA's price is $68 and the option's strike price is $70. This option is still OTM and has no intrinsic value. No one will exercise this call option and, therefore, the investor can keep the options premium (worth a total of $5.85*500=$2,925) and keep her shares of BABA. In this situation, the investor's total cash flow is $2,925-$915=$2,010. Compared to the cash outflow in the previous *WITHOUT* scenario, total cash flow with the covered call options strategy is +$2,010. Hence, we see that even in a slightly bearish market, investors can generate additional revenues by renting stocks in their portfolios.

< 87 >

Table 7.3: *Benefits of "Stock Rental" in Bullish Markets*

BABA increases from $69.83 to $70 per share.	
WITHOUT the covered call strategy	In this case, the investor will happily earn the profits generated from the increase in BABA stock price: ($70-$69.83)*500=$85.
WITH the covered call strategy	Now the BABA stock price is the same as the strike price. This call option is ATM. However, the option has zero intrinsic value. No one will exercise this call option and, therefore, the investor can still keep the options premium (worth a total of $5.85*500=$2,925) and keep her shares of BABA.
	In addition, the investor also gains $70-$69.83=$0.17 per share because she owns the stock. Further more, the total cash flow on the BABA stock holding is $0.17*500=$85. Therefore, the investor's total cash flow is $2,925+$85=$3,010.
	Compared to the cash flow in the previous *WITHOUT* scenario, total cash flow with the covered call options strategy is $3,010. Hence, we see that in a slightly bullish market, investors can generate additional revenues by renting stocks in their portfolios.

In summary, savvy investors can benefit from utilizing the covered call options strategy to "rent" their stock – in both bullish and bearish markets.

7.2 RISKS OF THE COVERED CALL OPTIONS STRATEGY

No trading strategy can guarantee that an investor will generate profits 100% of the time; that includes the covered call options strategy. In Table 7.4, we examine some potential risks investors may face when utilizing the covered call options strategy. In this table, we will only illustrate the most significant risk investors may face; others will be described in Section 7.3. The example in Table 7.4 illustrates that an investor can lose some potential profits from the appreciation of holding the underlying assets when utilizing the covered call options strategy.

< 88 >

Table 7.4: *Risks of the Covered Call Options Strategy*

BABA increases from $69.83 to $78 per share.	
WITHOUT the covered call strategy	In this case, the investor will happily earn the profits generated from the increase in BABA stock price: ($78-$69.83)*500=$4,085.
WITH the covered call strategy	So now, BABA's stock price is $78 and the option's strike price is still $70. Unfortunately, the investor is on the wrong side of the market when she chose this call option.

This call option is ITM and will be exercised. But, fortunately, the investor has the shares of BABA stock in her portfolio. Hence, she has to sell her BABA stock for $70 per share even though they are worth $78 per share.

So, if the investor bought the shares for $69.83 per share and sold them at $70 per share she will only gain $0.17 for each share. The investor's total earnings from appreciation of BABA is $0.17*500=$85 plus $2,925 option premium. Hence, this yields a total cash flow of $2,925+$85=$3,010 to the investor.

Compared to the $4,085 cash flow in the previous *WITHOUT* scenario, the total cash flow with the covered call options strategy is only $3,010. Therefore, in this case, the investor will not be a "happy camper."

Note: As discussed in Scenario #5 of Section 6.3, the investor may consider closing the covered call options positions in this very bullish case. |

< 89 >

7.3 SWOT ANALYSIS FOR THE COVERED CALL OPTIONS STRATEGY

A SWOT analysis is commonly applied in business planning. This methodology allows you to easily identify factors that may have influence in the achievement of your goals, as well as to assess their effects. Since the influence of each factor may be positive or negative and they are both internal and external to a business, these factors may be sorted into four categories, organized in the so-called SWOT matrix or box. The SWOT box is a 4 by 4 matrix where one can group the factors classified as inner or environmental and advantageous or disadvantageous to reach a goal. (Pahl and Richter, 2007), (Investopedia)

In accordance with the subject of this book, our business deals with writing covered call options and our general goal lies in obtaining the highest revenue from the money invested in our portfolio. The SWOT components – to be discussed in subsections 7.3.1 through 7.3.4 – are as follows:

- ❖ **S**trengths of the covered call options strategy
- ❖ **W**eaknesses of the covered call options strategy
- ❖ **O**pportunities of the covered call options strategy
- ❖ **T**hreats of the covered call options strategy

7.3.1 STRENGTHS OF THE COVERED CALL OPTIONS STRATEGY

> *Covered Call Options Strategy is one of the most profitable low-risk investment strategies.*

- ❖ It is one of the most profitable low-risk investment strategies.
- ❖ It requires no margin since the underlying asset covers the options sold.
- ❖ It's a relatively low-risk options strategy that allows you to generate additional income on a stock that you already own.
- ❖ It can be used to create downside protection and manage risk in your portfolio.
- ❖ It allows investors to capture all corporate dividends.

< 90 >

❖ For an IRA retirement account, the biggest advantage of writing covered calls is the tax benefit that comes with it. When you make money through a covered call strategy in your IRA retirement account, the IRS doesn't tax your profits on an annual basis as it would in a traditional brokerage account. As a result, when you retire, you don't have to pay taxes on the covered call income you generated, assuming you've held your account for at least 5 years and perhaps with some additional limitations -- depending on the type of IRA account you have. (Epstein, 2016)

❖ It can change an altogether aggressive speculation to a conservative investment.

❖ It can be used in most market conditions.

❖ Investors can still vote as a shareholder.

7.3.2 WEAKNESSES OF THE COVERED CALL OPTIONS STRATEGY

❖ Potential profit is limited to the strike price of the option.

❖ Big gains in short amount of time may not always be possible.

❖ Give up the right to future stock price appreciation.

❖ There's a significant learning curve and time commitment in learning how to use the covered call options strategy.

❖ May not be suitable for investors who hold stocks for a short period of time.

❖ Premiums may generate much less income if the expiration date is not far off. However, long-term options have more market risk.

❖ Depending on the astuteness of the trader, a relatively large portfolio may be needed in order to trade covered calls effectively; otherwise, broker fees will eat up your profits.

Big gains in short amount of time may not always be possible.

< 91 >

7.3.3 OPPORTUNITIES OF THE COVERED CALL OPTIONS STRATEGY

30-35% of option contracts expire worthless.

❖ Investors can expect an initial cash inflow into their accounts.
❖ It works well for long investment horizons.
❖ With the right trading tools, investors can make extra money from home (even while trading in their pajamas, on the beach, in airports, etc.) -- instead of just "hoping and praying" that the price of the stocks in their portfolio will go up.
❖ 30-35% of option contracts expire worthless.
❖ The covered call options strategy is conservative enough that it's allowed within an IRA and other tax-deferred retirement plans.

7.3.4 THREATS OF THE COVERED CALL OPTIONS STRATEGY

Investors can lose extensive potential profits when stock prices increase sharply.

❖ It's more appropriate for steady gains and income generation; hence, it may not be ideal for investors looking to make outsized gains in a short period of time.
❖ Investors are vulnerable to positive surprises in the market.
❖ Investors can lose extensive potential profits when stock prices increase sharply.
❖ Investors can lose some flexibility in the management of their assets.
❖ For relatively novice investors, it may be tough to initially figure out which call options pay decent premiums.

In summary, a SWOT matrix adapted to the business dealing with covered call options can be found in Figure 7.2.

< 92 >

Figure 7.2: **SWOT Analysis for the Covered Call Options Strategy**

STRENGTH

Advantageous inner factors
- Profitable Low-Risk Investment Strategy
- No Margin Requirement
- Additional Income from Stocks You Owned
- Can Provide Downside Protection
- Can Capture Stock Dividends
- Tax Benefits for IRA Retirement Account
- Conservative Investment Strategy
- Widely Usable
- Investors Still Have Vote Right

WEAKNESS

Disadvantageous inner factors
- Potential Profits are Limited
- Not Always Fast Money
- Time Consuming for Learning the Covered Call Strategy
- Not Always Suitable for Short Term Investment
- Not Always Huge Profits
- May Require Fairly Large Portfolio

S W O T

OPPORTUNITY

Advantageous environmental factors
- Initial Cash Inflow
- Perfect for Long-Term Investment
- 30-35% of Option Contracts Expire Worthless
- Option Strategy Allowed Within IRA

THREAT

Disadvantageous environmental factors
- No Fast and Large Profits
- Vulnerable to Bullish Market
- Lose Potential Profits under Bullish Market
- Lose Flexibility
- Should Consider Opportunity Cost
- Need to Find the Call Option With Decent Premium

< 93 >

As long as the above considerations are taken into account, the covered call options strategy may be an excellent low-risk trading technique to utilize to generate extra income. In addition, according to statistics published by the Chicago Board Options Exchange (CBOE), we would like to emphasize the fact that 30 to 35% of traded options expire worthless each year. This key fact - listed as one of the opportunities in our SWOT analysis (Figure 7.2) – is good news indeed for a covered call writer. If the covered call is not exercised, the option seller can simply pocket the options premium and retain his shares of the underlying stock. (Chicago Board Options Exchange), (Ellman, 2015)

The covered call options strategy will allow low-risk profile investors to exploit the full profit potential of their shares, instead of just holding them in a "dormant" state. This bulletproof trading strategy is analogous to real estate investors leasing property in exchange for an acceptable rent payment.

7.4 CHAPTER WRAP-UP

In this chapter, we discussed the following:

- ❖ The most significant benefits of the covered calls option strategy.
- ❖ The most significant potential risks faced by covered call option strategy users.
- ❖ A SWOT Analysis to explain other factors that may have influence on the performance of covered call options strategy.

< 94 >

REFERENCES

Chicago Board Options Exchange, www.cboe.com/

Ellman, Alan, "Percentage of Options Expiring Worthless: Debunking a Myth," *The Blue Collar Investor*, http://www.thebluecollarinvestor.com/, 2015.

Epstein, Lita, *How Much Are Taxes on an IRA Withdrawal?*, http://www.investopedia.com/articles/personal-finance/021015/how-much-are-taxes-ira-withdrawal.asp, 2016.

Investopedia, "SWOT Analysis," www.Investopedia.com

Pahl, Nadine and A. Richter, *SWOT Analysis. Idea, Methodology and a Practical Approach*, http://www.grin.com/en/e-book/124554/swot-analysis-idea-methodology-and-a-practical-approach, 2007.

< 95 >

INDEX

Locators with 't' are tables and locators with 'f' are figures.

< 96 >

Locators with 't' are tables and locators with 'f' are figures.

< 97 >

Locators with 't' are tables and locators with 'f' are figures.

< 98 >

Made in the USA
Middletown, DE
30 January 2017